Recruiting and Training Volunteers

The Adult Education Association Professional Development Series

CONSULTING EDITORS

Don F. Seaman, *Texas A&M University*

Alan R. Pardoen, *Mankato State University*

BUILDING THE LITERATURE OF A PROFESSION

About twenty-five years ago, between 1955 and 1959, the Adult Education Association developed a popular series of pamphlets to provide guidance to practitioners responsible for designing and delivering educational services to adults. At that time, it was recognized that many teachers, group leaders, and administrators working directly with adults had no training in the field of adult education, and few even knew that such training was available.

Rapid expansion has occurred in adult education since the inception of the old series. Institutions have responded enthusiastically and imaginatively to adults' increasing demands for programs. In addition, there has been significant development of the literature on the needs and interests of adults and on programming techniques to meet the needs of the adult student.

The expansion of the literature, the new clientele groups, and the increased number of participants created the need for a new series of publications which would be of value to those who serve on the firing line, working directly with adult learners on a day-to-day basis.

Although training programs in adult education have increased, they have not kept pace with the expanding field. Many of those employed in adult education are not aware that there is a growing body of knowledge and techniques which can help them perform their role better. Many are not even aware that they are functioning as "adult educators."

The AEA Professional Development Series is a cooperative effort of the Adult Education Association and the McGraw-Hill Book Company. The first titles were released in the fall of 1980. Each publication takes a practical, "how to," approach, with philosophical and theoretical considerations enhancing and lending support to the practical side of the content. Frequent examples, case studies, and critical incidents demonstrate the application of information, enabling the reader to perceive how an idea may be put to use in an on-the-job situational context.

The intended audience for the series is the administrator, teacher, or counselor who is faced with the day-to-day responsibility of providing educational services to an adult population, and the aspiring adult educator currently engaged in a formal training program in preparation for assuming a role as an adult education leader.

The Series
Boyle: Planning Better Programs
Seaman: Working Effectively with Task-Oriented Groups
Ilsley and Niemi: Recruiting and Training Volunteers

Recruiting and Training Volunteers

Paul J. Ilsley
John A. Niemi

Northern Illinois University

McGraw-Hill Book Company

New York   St. Louis   San Francisco   Auckland   Bogotá   Hamburg
Johannesburg   London   Madrid   Mexico   Montreal   New Delhi
Panama   Paris   São Paulo   Singapore   Sydney   Tokyo   Toronto

To Judy and Muriel

This book was set in Times Roman by David Seham Associates.
The editors were Donald W. Burden and James B. Armstrong;
the production supervisor was Diane Renda.
R. R. Donnelley & Sons Company was printer and binder.

RECRUITING AND TRAINING VOLUNTEERS

1234567890 DODO 89876543210

Library of Congress Cataloging in Publication Data

Ilsley, Paul J
    Recruiting and training volunteers.

    (The Adult Education Association professional
development series)
    Bibliography: p.
    Includes index.
    1. Volunteer workers in education. 2. Adult
education—United States. 3. Volunteer workers
in social service. I. Niemi, John A., joint author.
II. Title. III. Series: Adult Education Association. Adult Education Association professional
development series.
LB2844.I44   374   80-19693
ISBN 0-07-000556-7

Contents

Preface

The 1980s promise continued emphasis on lifelong learning. Hence, for the remainder of this century, adult educators will confront enormous challenges. The learning needs of relatively well-educated adults will continue to grow, with demands for programs to help them fulfill new roles, adjust to new life styles, and update competencies. But the greatest challenge will relate to the acute learning needs of a vast army of adults who face severe job and social limitations as a result of their low level of education.

Obviously, it is impossible for professionals and part-time adult educators to tackle such huge tasks alone. Here, the utilization of volunteers, who possess rich and varied backgrounds of experience, represents a viable, indeed crucial, source of help. Interestingly enough, Alexis de Tocqueville, the perceptive Frenchman who visited our shores more than a century ago, articulated the value of reliance on voluntary action as early as 1835. In his book *Democracy in America*, he wrote:

> In no country in the world has the principle of association been more successfully used or applied to a greater multitude of objects than in America. Beside the permanent associations which are established by law . . . a vast number of others are

formed and maintained by the agency of primary individuals. . . . In the United States, associations are established to promote the public safety, commerce, industry, morality, and religion. There is no end which the human will despairs of attaining through the combined power of individuals united in a society.

The purpose of this book is to provide adult educators with a sequential approach that they can follow (1) when determining how volunteers might be introduced into existing programs and (2) when planning future programs in which volunteers will form a vital component. This book fills a hiatus in the literature of adult education. It does so by leading adult educators who wish to capitalize on the talents of volunteers through the process—from the initial decision to use volunteers to the final step of evaluating their performance as seasoned workers in a program.

The authors are indebted to Dr. Muriel Thomkins Niemi for her critical comments on the organization and editing of this volume.

Paul J. Ilsley
John A. Niemi

What Is Voluntarism?

INTRODUCTION

According to a Census Bureau survey, nearly 37 million Americans engaged in some form of volunteer work in 1974. This figure represented one of four Americans over the age of 13.[1] In order to better understand this phenomenon, it is important to examine the concept of voluntarism.

Voluntarism embodies a spirit of willingness (even eagerness) on the part of volunteers to contribute their time and energies without remuneration and a willingness on the part of paid personnel to collaborate with volunteers in a particular setting. As a movement which has developed spontaneously in American society, voluntarism has enjoyed recognition as a bona fide activity. The types of activity have been described by David Horton Smith, a leading author in the field, as (1) service-oriented activities; (2) issue- or cause-oriented activities; (3) activities for self-expression, such as sports groups and dinner clubs; (4) activities for occupa-

---

[1] *Americans Volunteer,* ACTION (The Agency for Volunteer Service), Washington, D.C., 1975.

tional and economic self-interest, such as professional groups and unions; and (5) activities for philanthropic and fundraising purposes.[2] In this book, only the first two types will be explored. No attempt will be made to deal with the other three categories of voluntary activity.

In service-oriented activities, adult educators make extensive use of volunteers, placing them in a number of roles, e.g., tutors and support staff assisting others in coping with problems. The issue- or cause-oriented activities might be labeled "advocacy voluntarism," whereby volunteers work to make community agencies and individuals aware of a need for social change. In both cases, the volunteers' commitment is based largely on a sense of duty associated with bettering their fellow human beings, a course of action which enriches their own lives. It is important to point out that any attempt to establish a dichotomy between service and advocacy voluntarism is a false one, as undoubtedly there are elements of both in all volunteer-based organizations.

Another way to categorize the activities of voluntarism would be by fields of service, which include the following:

- Civic affairs—e.g., League of Women Voters
- Communications—e.g., public-access cable TV franchise
- Cultural and spiritual activities—e.g., county historical museum, churches
- Education—e.g., Literacy Volunteers of America, Inc.
- Environmental affairs—e.g., Nader's raiders
- Parks and recreation—e.g., camp directors, youth coordinators
- Physical and mental health—e.g., candy stripers, rape crisis intervention centers
- Social justice—e.g., Alinsky community advocates
- Social welfare—e.g., YMCA, YWCA, Chicago's Hull House

THE NEED FOR VOLUNTEERS

Today, many adult education agencies need additional staff for educational outreach services. Through the use of volunteers, assistance can be sought from persons who can make additional contributions because of their special life experiences and strong community identity.

The need for volunteers is directly related to the increased commitment by adults to learning as a lifelong process. As far as the disadvantaged segment of the adult population is concerned, many members require writing, computation, and other life skills in order to function in the

---

[2]David Horton Smith, "Research and Communication Needs in Voluntary Action," in John G. Cull and Richard E. Hardy (eds.), *Volunteerism: An Emerging Profession*, Charles C Thomas, Publisher, Springfield, Ill., 1974.

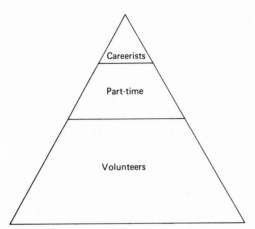

Figure 1-1 Houle's typology of leadership.

larger society and even to prepare them to become lifelong learners. Given the number of adults in this country who are unable to function effectively due to these deficiencies, there is a growing realization that professional and part-time adult educators cannot do the task alone and need the assistance of volunteer tutors.[3]

Volunteers can provide other invaluable services in an adult education organization. By adding volunteers, programs have often fostered better public awareness of and support for their goals, enriched and enlarged services to students and clients, and made possible the expansion of services to meet the educational and cultural needs of a changing adult population. The decision to use volunteers in numerous roles (e.g., public relations, funding drives, teaching, nursing, social work) has proved important to libraries, museums, schools, hospitals, churches, synagogues, cultural organizations, universities, and other institutions.

In the 1950s and 1960s, when the number of full-time professionals was small, the influence of volunteers in the field of adult education was enormous and diverse in scope. An awareness of the importance of volunteers to adult education was articulated by Cyril Houle. His model (Figure 1-1) represents a pyramid of leadership, the base of which contains the largest group of adult educators—the volunteers. Houle's pyramid includes two smaller groups—part-time adult educators at the intermediate level and full-time adult educators (professionals) at the apex. The model illustrates the numerical size of the three groups and shows that full-time staff could not function without the aid of part-time workers and volun-

[3]The 1970 census reported 54,330,000 people 16 years of age and older who had not completed high school and were not enrolled in school. *A Target Population in Adult Education,* National Advisory Council on Adult Education, Washington, D.C., 1974, p. 153.

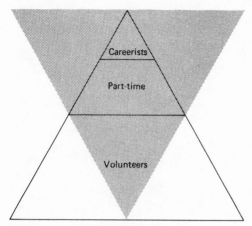

Figure 1-2 Typology of leadership.

teers.[4] By implication, it points to the responsibility that full-time staff bear to provide the training necessary for part-time workers and volunteers to fulfill their roles. That responsibility can best be shown by an inverted triangle (Figure 1-2) superimposed on Houle's pyramid. The triangle signifies the amount of preparation that full-time, part-time, and volunteer staff need in order to discharge their responsibilities.

MYTHS AND FEARS ABOUT VOLUNTEERS

Despite the obvious advantages of using volunteers, there persist among adult educators and other agency personnel certain myths and fears that cause them to resist the idea of incorporating volunteers into a program. It must be recognized that where myths and fears abound, there is usually an element of truth, or an underlying cause. The challenge of dealing realistically with those concerns, while cherishing the spirit of voluntarism, is perhaps the most difficult one to face in a decision to use volunteers. The list of concerns appearing below is not exhaustive, but includes those which professionals most frequently express concerning volunteers.

  1 *Volunteers may take the jobs of professionals.* This threat is notable in occupations troubled by a shrinking labor market. The argument runs that volunteers do jobs which should be remunerated; furthermore, if they perform without pay the same work others perform for pay, staff bargaining power (especially in part-time settings) will be reduced. It is

[4]Cyril O. Houle, "The Education of Adult Education Leaders," in Malcolm S. Knowles (ed.), *Handbook of Adult Education in the United States,* Adult Education Association of the U.S.A., Chicago, 1960, pp. 119–120.

feared that the presence of volunteers will be cited as a reason for cutting salaries, withholding legitimate pay increases, or eliminating jobs entirely.

In response to this concern, the introduction of volunteer activity creates more paid staff positions, not fewer, because of the need for paid personnel to organize that activity. In addition, where the involvement of volunteers draws attention to significant social issues, a result might be the funding of new paid positions. In other words, volunteers tend to supplement rather than supplant paid positions. Rarely are they expected to duplicate the roles of professional personnel. Moreover, volunteer support permits paid staff to achieve more in the time available to them and to pay more attention to other aspects of their roles.

2 *Volunteers have questionable motives.* They are charged, variously, with being do-gooders, perpetual crusaders, status seekers, and ego trippers who use the role of volunteer in quest of power. Frequently they are accused of using this role to overcome guilt feelings and to meet unfulfilled personal needs.

In response, it is certain that volunteers entertain many different motives, or combinations of motives, and that these might be extremely complex. It is the task of a volunteer coordinator to identify the motives of volunteers, in order to determine their suitability for roles within an agency. Motives commonly represent personal needs, and these can be openly discussed. It is not enough that a person wants to volunteer. The needs of the client or student must be considered with those of volunteers. It is hoped that no volunteer would be placed in a situation where the values conflict with his or her values, capabilities, or wishes.

3 *Volunteers want to become involved in exciting and challenging tasks.* They will avoid routine, yet essential, details such as record keeping, follow-up activities, lesson planning, or tasks that appear too demeaning.

In response to this concern, the situation can be averted if new volunteers understand, at the outset, that every job has routine aspects that must be dealt with. However, it is incumbent upon a volunteer coordinator to place a volunteer in a job that is both compatible with his or her expertise and challenging. If the latter criterion cannot be met, a coordinator should be forthright about telling prospective volunteers that an agency cannot offer the stimulating tasks they seek.

4 *Volunteers lack commitment and tend to be "here today, gone tomorrow."* Lacking persistence and continuity of purpose, they are seen as unable to develop the dedication of professionals and will not be as effective with clients.

In response to this concern, it is unrealistic to assume that all volunteers will internalize the norms and long-term commitment of professional staff. However, proper orientation, training, and management should increase their dedication. Of particular importance is the creation of a sense of purpose and a learning environment that is open, friendly, and stimulating. It is well to remember that, at times, a reasonable flow of volunteers in and out of an agency can have a revitalizing effect.

5 *Volunteers are difficult to manage.* According to this argument, they assume too much influence or power with the clients or want to do things in their own way, whether it is appropriate or not. Moreover, being part-time and unpaid, volunteers cannot be fired or even evaluated; hence they are not accountable to the same extent as paid staff.

In response, these fears can be laid to rest by the establishment of well-organized volunteer programs. There is no reason why irresponsible or inept volunteers cannot be reprimanded or fired. As for competent volunteers, they would probably welcome evaluation, especially if they aspire to full-time employment in the future.

6 *Volunteers present a loyalty threat.* For example, they are more likely to censure agency activities or to breach confidentiality.

The response to this concern is that, on the contrary, volunteers appear to be advocates of programs they join. As for criticisms they advance, where these are constructive, they form a valuable source of new insights from the public sector. Such insights can help in assessing the strengths and weaknesses of a program and in interpreting it to a wider audience.

THE SETTING FOR VOLUNTARISM

During the 1960s, adult educators paid less attention than before to the use of volunteers. However, during the 1970s, voluntarism as a movement witnessed a noticeable degree of maturity. A partial listing of volunteer associations which developed during the past decade appears in Appendix A.

In adult education, the settings for voluntarism are described by means of Schroeder's typology of adult education agencies and organizations.[5]

Adult education agencies: Type I   Educational organizations in which serving adults is a *primary* purpose.

Historically, agencies in this first group have included business schools, correspondence schools, technical schools, and other schools that are independently financed, operated for profit, and designed to provide adults with a myriad of curricular offerings, e.g., courses to improve basic skills, programs to develop vocational talents, activities to stimulate new avocational interests, and so forth.

More recently, the flourishing of nontraditional education has resulted in a virtual explosion of new nonprofit educational organizations oriented to the adult learner. They carry a variety of names—free universities, store-front schools, alternative educational facilities, learning exchanges, and educational centers. Some operate residential programs; others do not. Some offer credit; others do not. The characteristics and

[5] Wayne L. Schroeder, "Adult Education Defined and Described," in Robert M. Smith et al. (eds.), *Handbook of Adult Education,* Macmillan and Adult Education Association of the U.S.A., New York, 1970, pp. 25–43.

offerings of newer Type I adult education agencies are remarkably diverse. Given the varied needs of adult learners and the still evolving principles and theories of adult education, that is probably as it should be.

Adult education agencies: Type II Educational organizations in which serving adults is a *secondary* purpose.

Agencies in this second group include three kinds of formal educational organizations—public school districts, 2-year community colleges, and 4-year public and private colleges and universities—that have historically viewed children and youth as their focal clientele, but have also tried to provide minimal educational opportunities for adults. Each has been involved in its own way in adult education, sponsoring communitywide educational activities, operating adult evening programs, conducting special workshops and conferences for adults, and so on. Also traditionally included in this group has been the Department of Agriculture's Cooperative Extension Service, which has provided a breadth of educational opportunities for adults, ranging from individual consultation and information services to extensive course offerings and expanded uses of mass media to disseminate information.

Adult education agencies: Type III Noneducational organizations in which adult education is an implicit part of their broad purposes.

Museums, libraries, and social service organizations are good examples of agencies in this third group. Although they are not considered educational organizations in the same sense as schools and colleges, all three provide valuable educational services to both the general public and specific adult clienteles. For instance, through their extensive resources, collections, displays, lectures, and tours, museums and libraries furnish adults with a vast array of opportunities for lifelong learning. In addition, many libraries demonstrate their interest in adult education by sponsoring literacy tutoring programs and providing videotape GED programs for high school dropouts; by extending their outreach programs and establishing special collections of print and nonprint materials in branch library facilities; by offering concerts, discussion programs, and film seminars; and by serving as brokers between adults who have special kinds of educational needs and other adults who have the competencies and interests to meet those needs. Finally, in addition to disseminating information about their specific services, many health agencies offer regular programs for adults on alcoholism, accident prevention, and family life, and many welfare agencies work regularly with adults who want to develop the knowledge, skills, and attitudes necessary to escape economic disadvantage.

Adult education agencies: Type IV Noneducational organizations which provide adult education, but in which adult education is subordinate to other purposes.

Agencies in this fourth group include churches, business and industrial concerns, labor unions, professional organizations, and voluntary associations. In each case, the agency's reason for being is not primarily educational activities oriented to adults. For instance, churches provide both religious and secular services, special meetings, and discussions of topics of current theological and secular interest. Both industrial and business concerns, as well as labor unions and professional organizations, develop and sponsor a host of educational activities designed to provide leadership training for members, increase on-the-job competence, improve labor-management relations, and so forth. Nearly every voluntary association, whether oriented to national, state, or local issues, organizes and carries out an educational campaign directed at least to its members and often to the general public.

Figure 1-3 summarizes the typology of adult education agencies in a two-dimensional matrix, in which the educational or noneducational nature of an organization is related to its degree of commitment to adult education as one of its purposes.

Nature of the organization

		Educational	Noneducational
Degree of commitment to adult education as a purpose of the organization	Providing educational opportunities for adults is an explicit, primary purpose of the organization	*Type I agencies* (for example, business, correspondence, technical, and other proprietary schools; and the full range of alternative nontraditional schools and agencies)	
	Providing educational opportunities for adults is an implicit, secondary purpose of the organization	*Type II agencies* (for example, public school districts; 2-year community colleges; Cooperative Extension Services; and 4-year colleges and universities)	*Type III agencies* (for example, museums, libraries, and health and welfare agencies)
	Providing educational opportunities for adults is subordinate to other purposes of the organization		*Type IV agencies* (for example, churches, business and industrial concerns, labor unions, professional organizations, and voluntary associations)

Figure 1-3 Distinguishing among four types of adult education agencies.

CONCLUSION

Voluntarism is an important and growing concept in the United States today. Its roots are as old as the country itself, and the historical development of voluntarism parallels the growth of the nation. Most myths and fears about utilizing volunteers can be quickly countered through common sense and by citing the experiences of successful volunteer programs. Adult volunteers can be found in almost every type of agency or organization in which education plays a role. In essence, voluntarism is more needed today than ever before in our complex, dynamic society.

Chapter 2

Organizational Factors That Influence the Use of Volunteers

INTRODUCTION

Often a decision to use volunteers in existing adult education programs is based on pragmatic considerations. For example, a rapidly growing program might encounter difficulty in staffing and recognize its need for volunteers. As pointed out in Chapter 1, many adult education organizations form part of a larger organization whose overall goals include adult education as a secondary, or marginal, activity. Consequently, funding, staffing, and facilities are often limited. For established adult education programs, a decision to use volunteers might culminate in the selection of volunteer paraprofessionals to fill such roles as counselors or tutors. Or, support staff might be recruited for administrative work—typing, filing, and logistical assignments such as promotion and transportation. Sometimes an adult educator responsible for planning programs will decide to plan an outreach program whose purposes can best be achieved by selecting indigenous volunteers from a community. The services of such persons have been found to be an effective resource for meeting certain community needs.

Any plan to utilize volunteers in an adult education organization by the adult educator (who may act as a volunteer coordinator) must begin with an understanding of the factors that facilitate or inhibit decisions. In this instance, the vital factors are the mission or purpose of an organization and its goals, objectives, and fiscal support.

FACTORS THAT AFFECT DECISION MAKING

A decision represents an attempt to solve a problem by making a choice. Seldom is it a choice between "right" and "wrong," but among several alternatives that offer varying advantages and disadvantages. For example, a new adult education program in need of counselors might decide to recruit a major portion of staff from volunteers belonging to the ranks of retired professionals. It is important for any decision to be acceptable not only to the volunteer coordinator but also to the rest of the administration and the staff. Here, personal factors that influence decisions must not be overlooked. To illustrate, where volunteers display physical handicaps, their potential value to an organization may not be fully appreciated. Or, a potential volunteer may have had youthful experiences, such as serving a prison sentence, which are considered undesirable. Such persons tend to be excluded because of their prior deviant behavior; yet they may be the very persons whose insights are most needed in the planning of a particular program.

Equally important in a decision to utilize volunteers are situational factors that relate to an organization's concept of both paid staff roles and volunteer roles. For example, if the prevailing expectations held by paid male staff toward women volunteers have been expressed in the design of low-level volunteer positions, the result would likely be the exploitation or denigration of volunteers. Another example of a situational factor would be a conviction, on the part of some persons in an organization, that volunteers' roles must "fit" with the roles of professional staff. Such a view, which supports a superordinate-subordinate relationship between the two groups, is inappropriate today and threatens the humanistic underpinnings of adult education. The implied warning is that in any decision to utilize volunteers in an organization, it is wise to avoid narrowly based personal factors and to seek, instead, an overall operating philosophy, sometimes referred to as mission or purpose.

MISSION OR PURPOSE OF AN ORGANIZATION

Any attempt to analyze the personal and situational factors at work in a decision to utilize volunteers in an organization must begin with a review of its mission or purpose, which forms part of its "grand design." The other components of a grand design are creed, goals, specific objectives arranged in a hierarchy, and the necessary fiscal support.[1]

A creed or a broad statement of intended relationships (a "mission statement") is meant to appeal to all groups—staff, clients, and the general public. It may be especially appealing to volunteers if it embodies ideals with which they can identify. For example, the initial appeal of the Peace Corps and VISTA lay in the opportunities presented to volunteers to transform their altruistic ideals into action.

The mission or purpose relates to the operating philosophy of an organization. As Peter Drucker asserts, such a statement begins by providing "common vision, common understanding, and unity of direction,"[2] all of which help to determine "what the efforts of the organization are, what it will be, and what it should be."[3]

Today, many adult education organizations are revising their statements in order to reach larger segments of society. Instead of relying on a centralized campus or other educational facilities which generally appeal to younger, highly educated professionals, such organizations are turning to outreach facilities to make possible the participation of other adults—those with low incomes, the aged, single parents, and so on. Other adult education organizations are revising their statements so that volunteers are seen as a major resource in the delivery of adult basic education programs. For example, in Programmed Activities for Correctional Education (PACE) at Chicago's Cook County Jail, volunteer tutors play important roles in helping inmate students progress with their basic education studies.

Clearly, an imperative need exists for an organization to examine and reexamine its grand design, especially its statement, to ensure that it is keeping abreast of current needs in a community and among its own paid staff and volunteers. Lacking such direction, an organization is in danger of becoming static and losing its vision and unified sense of purpose. If such renewal does not occur, past experiences and present contingencies will predominate in the setting of new goals. Under these circumstances, the vital task of goal setting will sink to the level of a haphazard, reactive process.

GOALS

After articulating a mission statement, the next step is setting long-range goals. These furnish an organization with a guide that gives direction and

---

[1]Charles H. Granger, "The Hierarchy of Objectives," *Harvard Business Review,* May–June, 1964.

[2]Peter F. Drucker, *Management: Tasks, Responsibilities, and Practices,* Harper and Row, New York, 1974, p. 77.

[3]Ibid., p. 94.

stimulates action. In an organization that plans to utilize volunteers, goals respond to needs or problems enunciated by groups of citizens or, more generally, by a community.

Service Goals

It is evident that organizations engaged with similar problems often interpret their missions differently and, accordingly, set different goals. This phenomenon is illustrated in the provision of educational opportunities for the aged. One approach has an organization design programs for the aged around the regular array of course offerings, without taking into account the older adults' orientation to life, based on physical condition, experiences, life styles, and commitments. Specifically a 2-year college had an outreach program for aged blind adults focus chiefly on recreation and ignore intellectual stimulation. A second approach has an organization collaborate actively with the elderly in determining their own needs and, on that basis, design programs aptly suited to the demands of later life. This process produces a set of goals that are quite different from those formulated in the first approach. To return to the example relating to aged blind adults, a collaborative approach would involve them in clarifying their special needs and in developing a program that might stress contemporary issues in the community and elsewhere. It is important to note that neither approach should be judged "right" or "wrong." In some situations, the structured institutional approach described first may be preferable. In other cases, a collaborative approach would be appropriate.

The mission and goals of an organization also supply direction for the planning of educational programs. If a service organization had as its mission the design and delivery of adult basic education programs to single parents with low incomes, the goal would be to provide certain courses as a prerequisite for job training. However, this goal may be understood differently by students, instructors, volunteer tutors, and prospective employers. The students may view the course content as irrelevant to job training, while the instructor may consider it necessary remedial work. The volunteer tutors may find themselves somewhere between these perceived goals. Finally, the prospective employers may have little appreciation of the importance of basic skills as a prerequisite for job training. If it proves unappealing to some persons, this goal might produce little in the way of meaningful results. The lesson to be drawn is that an organization should review a goal in light of different perceptions of it. Although a goal might remain unchanged, the clearer understanding gained of factors affecting a goal both within and outside an organization could culminate in more unified efforts toward achieving a goal. Moreover, supplementary goals could be established. For example, data about the low completion rate of single, low-income parents enrolled in a program might reveal an inability to concentrate on a course of study because of problems associated with babysitting, transportation, or money for books and supplies. A supplementary goal would consist of the establishment of ancillary services, staffed with volunteers in conjunction with the educational program, to perform the services needed by the low-income parents.

Advocacy Goals

While the preceding example of goal setting relates chiefly to the service function of voluntarism, of equal importance are advocacy goals established by some organizations that utilize volunteers. The mission would be assisting community groups to act together in bringing to light problems that have been ignored by local governments or other groups responsible for the quality of life in a community. An example of an advocacy goal would be raising the critical consciousness of a community, a goal that poses both challenges and risks to an organization. In particular, the risks associated with threats to the power of certain groups must be well understood. Otherwise, advocacy goals might be construed not as ways to stimulate or guide people to take action, but as unrealistic, even obstructive, notions that would be dropped under pressure from social, economic, or political groups.

In summary, goals indicate to clients, paid staff, and volunteers an organization's plan to serve them, through the formation of either service goals or advocacy goals. Goals also indicate some boundaries concerning what an organization will or will not do.

OBJECTIVES

Having established long-range goals, the next step in developing a program to utilize volunteers is setting objectives. Unlike goals, which are statements of intent, objectives are specific, clearly defined components of a goal. Objectives are stated in measurable terms and are capable of being achieved within a reasonable period of time.

In short, setting objectives involves transforming goals into narrower, more specific units. Marlene Wilson suggests a system which will enable the staff of an organization to distinguish between goals and objectives. This system carries the acronym of SMAC, interpreted as follows:

S—Is it specific?
M—Is it measurable?
A—Is it achievable?
C—Is it compatible with the overall goals and other objectives [of an organization]?

[4]Marlene Wilson, *The Effective Management of Volunteer Programs,* Volunteer Management Associates, Boulder, Colo., 1976, p. 78.

Obviously, objectives should be operational in order to infuse an organization with a sense of commitment and direction. Well-defined objectives enable staff to utilize resources effectively in the mobilization of activities and to diminish the effects of constraints on carrying them through.

In any plan to utilize volunteers in an organization, it becomes apparent that there are two different types of objectives. The first set relates to building or expanding an organization, and it includes such items as roles and responsibilities of volunteers, recruitment, selection, training, placement, supervision, evaluation, and recognition. An example of the first set of objectives follows:

> A volunteer who has been added to a staff will demonstrate ability to show adult basic education students how to draw inferences.

The second set of objectives relates to the client who is going to be served and to decisions about how the utilization of volunteers will make possible the provision of desired services or the facilitation of community action through the process of advocacy. An example of the second set of objectives follows:

> A citizen in a community who has been trained to use a videotape recorder will create a position tape which depicts a community stand on an issue.

By setting specific objectives, an organization establishes a basis for determining whether the purpose of a particular activity has been achieved. This evaluative process, which describes changes or effects, is the topic of Chapter 8.

FISCAL SUPPORT

A decision to utilize volunteers in an organization requires careful scrutiny of fiscal support. Although volunteers work without pay, direct and indirect costs accrue in any program that solicits their services. Direct costs include insurance to cover volunteers in case of injury in job-related accidents. Other direct costs such as postage, telephone, training and working materials, travel allowances, and meals add up proportionately with each volunteer. Indirect costs for management and supervision, secretarial help, and extra heating and lighting can be substantial. Other funds may be needed to implement policies designed to build morale and strengthen the motivation of volunteers. Such policies include provision of child care, workshop and course tuition, professional development, resource materials, and awards for recognition.

It is emphasized that a realistic examination of present and potential funding is essential before any decision is made to utilize volunteers. No set rule could be stated to govern the amount of money that is needed, in light of the diversity of institutional goals, training programs, and management styles. However, a basic budget can be developed as a guide to the adequacy of fiscal support to achieve desired results. Where funds are inadequate, the alternatives may be to curtail a volunteer-based program, to acquire additional funds from sources within an organization, or to prepare a proposal or brief for the purpose of attracting funds from private and government sources.

CONCLUSION

A decision to utilize volunteers in an organization should not be made without understanding the factors that facilitate or inhibit the decision-making process. It is likewise important to have a firm grasp of an organization's grand design and mission which, translated into an operating philosophy, supply a common vision and a sense of unity. The broad, long-range goals that are generated provide direction to an organization. Specifically, they form the basis for setting objectives which are measurable and feasible during a time frame. It is emphasized that the entire planning process must be coupled with a realistic appraisal of the needed fiscal support.

If the factors outlined here are thoughtfully and systematically incorporated into an organization's plan to utilize volunteers, the first crucial stage in that process will be successfully completed. Further challenges to be faced and suggestions for overcoming them form the subject matter of subsequent chapters.

Chapter 3

Roles and Responsibilities of a Coordinator of Volunteers

INTRODUCTION

If the vacant position of volunteer coordinator were to be announced, the advertisement might read:

> Volunteer coordinator wanted; must have experience designing and implementing programs, working with organizations, preparing budgets, supervising volunteers, and maintaining records.

A detailed statement of responsibilities would specify assessment of the needs of an organization and of volunteers participating in its program; establishment of program goals and objectives; orientation of paid staff toward volunteers; job design; selection, recruitment, and orientation of volunteers; evaluation of a volunteer-based program and periodic reports about its progress; public relations regarding volunteer service; and development of linkages with other community agencies. Always, a volunteer coordinator is a central figure, a liaison between a volunteer-based program and the organization that houses it and between a program and a

17

Selected roles of a volunteer coordinator

			Administration						Training/ education				Counseling			Research/ evaluation		
			Program planner	Fiscal agent	Public relations agent	Liaison	Recruiter	Manager	Learner	Curriculum facilitator	Instructor	Media specialist	Diagnostician	Counselor	Placement sponsor	Observer	Record keeper	Evaluator
Selected program activities	Program design	Needs assessment	X		X								X				X	X
		Mission statement	X															X
		Establish goals and objectives	X	X													X	X
		Design of program components	X	X				X		X								X
		Obtaining facilities and materials		X				X						X				
		Creation of climate	X		X		X	X	X		X		X	X		X		
		Involvement of paid staff			X			X	X				X					
		Job design	X					X						X			X	
	Recruitment and selection	Recruitment	X					X									X	
		Application process			X		X		X			X		X				
		Interview						X	X		X		X			X		
		Selection agreement						X					X	X	X		X	X

Figure 3-1　Selected roles and responsibilities of a volunteer coordinator.

Selected roles of a volunteer coordinator

Selected program activities		Administration						Training/education				Counseling			Research/evaluation		
		Program planner	Fiscal agent	Public relations agent	Liaison	Recruiter	Manager	Learner	Curriculum facilitator	Instructor	Media specialist	Diagnostician	Counselor	Placement sponsor	Observer	Record keeper	Evaluator
Socialization and training	Orientation	X						X	X	X	X	X					
	Preservice training	X							X	X	X						X
	Placement						X		X				X				
	In-service training	X							X	X	X	X					X
Guidance	Motivation						X		X				X	X	X		X
	Supervision	X					X						X	X	X	X	X
	Recognition						X							X			
Administration	Management	X					X					X	X	X	X	X	X
	Evaluation		X				X						X			X	X
	Linkage development	X		X	X		X	X	X				X		X		X
	Continuing education							X	X								

Figure 3-1 *(Continued)*

community. As such, he or she is responsible for both ensuring the satisfaction of volunteers and achieving organizational goals related to a volunteer-based program.

It is recognized that the role will vary greatly from organization to organization and from program to program, depending upon the various goals and objectives, available resources, and other factors. For example, in many organizations, the position of volunteer is a salaried one. It is also recognized that not all programs assign equal weight to the same activities or equal status to a position. The responsibilities of a volunteer coordinator may vary as to their number, the emphasis accorded them, or the energy demanded in their performance. For example, in some organizations a volunteer coordinator might be heavily involved in developing goals and objectives, whereas in another, like a 4-H club program, he or she will encounter well-established goals and objectives. As for the varying emphasis on responsibilities, it seems likely that a volunteer coordinator in a crisis intervention center would have to put greater stress on preservice training than would be the case in a "meals-on-wheels" operation.

Despite the reservations stated above, it is possible to construct some guidelines for describing various roles of a volunteer coordinator. The approach taken in this chapter will be to discuss the selected roles in terms of selected responsibilities, which can best be examined in relation to activities typically associated with a volunteer-based program. Figure 3-1 attempts to match those responsibilities of a volunteer coordinator.

The activities appear under "Program design," "Recruitment and selection," "Socialization and training," "Guidance," and "Administration." The roles and responsibilities of a volunteer coordinator appear under "Administration," "Training/education," "Counseling," and "Research/evaluation." They testify to the considerable scope and diversity of the role as program planner, fiscal agent, public relations agent, liaison, recruiter, manager, learner, curriculum facilitator, instructor, media specialist, diagnostician, counselor, placement sponsor, observer, record keeper, and evaluator. Figure 3-2 outlines various tasks on a 13-month basis, the point being that certain activities should precede others. It is implied that the role of a volunteer coordinator changes as activities and tasks are completed.

PROGRAM DESIGN

Program design, which must always precede the recruitment of volunteers, will be discussed in eight parts: "Needs Assessment," "Mission Statement," "Establishing Goals and Objectives," "Design Program Components," "Obtaining Facilities and Materials," "Creation of Climate," "Involvement of Paid Staff," and "Job Design." Often, a volunteer coordinator is involved in such planning, which requires him or her to make many major decisions. For example, when a volunteer-based program is to be incorporated into an organization, the issue of compatibility must be addressed. Will the design and activities of the proposed program be compatible with the philosophy and rules of an organization with respect to recruitment, selection, and training of volunteers? To assist this process, care must be taken to keep paid staff and decision makers not merely informed of developments but actively involved in the initial planning and, later, in such activities as selection, supervision, and evaluation of volunteers.

Needs Assessment

Before the goals of a volunteer-based program can be specified, it is important to understand both organization and community needs. A volun-

Figure 3-2 *(Opposite)* Time-sequenced activities (based on calendar year).

Selected program activities

		Planning			Implementation				Active					
		M_1	M_2	M_3	M_4	M_5	M_6	M_7	M_8	M_9	M_{10}	M_{11}	M_{12}	M_1
Program design	Needs assessment	├────┤												
	Mission statement		├────┤											
	Establish goals and objectives		├────┤											
	Design of program components		├────┤											
	Obtaining facilities and materials		├────┤											
	Creation of climate			├──────────┤										
	Involvement of paid staff		├────────┤											
	Job design		├──────┤											
Recruitment and selection	Recruitment		├──────┤											
	Application process				├────┤									
	Interview					├────┤								
	Selection agreement					├──────┤								
Socialization and training	Orientation				├──────┤									
	Preservice training					├──────┤								
	Placement						├──────┤							
	In-service training							├──┤		├──┤			├──┤
Guidance	Motivation			├─────────────────────────────────┤										
	Supervision								├──────────────────┤					
	Recognition								├──────────────────┤					
Administration	Management	├──┤												
	Evaluation	├──┤												
	Linkage development	├──┤												
	Continuing education	├─┤	├─┤	├─┤	├─┤	├─┤	├─┤						

teer coordinator can obtain such information through surveys, visits with various community and organization leaders, and informal conversations and observations. In the pursuit of these activities, a volunteer coordinator becomes a public relations agent visible to the community and responsible for gaining the confidence of citizens, leaders, and decision makers in plans to utilize volunteers for a particular purpose. Simultaneously, he or she acts as an observer (or even a diagnostician) of organization and community needs, one who deliberately withholds the formulation of policy until the information-gathering process and analysis is complete.

Mission Statement

As discussed in Chapter 2, the statement provides a sense of mission for an organization. It presents an operating philosophy from which goals are established. These goals may seem unattainable in the short run—for example, to eradicate illiteracy, to eliminate prejudice, or to solve the housing needs of migrant workers.

Establishing Goals and Objectives

These are motivating factors that cause people to become and remain volunteers. Objectives are based on program goals, and are usually in more specific terms. A volunteer coordinator helps determine and fulfill program goals and objectives.

Design of Program Components

The design of program components addresses the question of how goals and objectives will be accomplished. For example, if one goal is to provide training for hospital volunteers, the appropriate component might be a series of preservice sessions on the topic of patient care. Selected roles, which are important for preplanning and are often overlooked, are shown in Figure 3-1. They include those of program planner, fiscal agent, manager, curriculum facilitator, and evaluator.

Obtaining Facilities and Materials

When implementing a program, a volunteer coordinator must make wise choices, based in part on the needs of volunteers, about such matters as distance from volunteers' homes, availability of food service, physical environment, materials, and equipment. Always, a volunteer coordinator must be mindful of the funds available for the program.

Creation of Climate

The psychological climate of a group (the topic of Chapter 4), includes prevailing attitudes within it—in this case, the attitudes of volunteers, their coordinator, and other program personnel. A climate manifests itself in the level of morale, the productivity of the program, and the satisfaction of volunteers' social needs. The climate is largely dependent upon a volunteer coordinator's leadership style and his or her skill in establishing and maintaining a high degree of trust and cooperation that will prove of mutual benefit to the organization and the volunteers.

Involvement of Paid Staff

A discussion of this activity assumes that a volunteer-based program will be incorporated into an organization. Essentially, the preparation of paid staff involves soliciting their support in the planning, conducting, and evaluation of a volunteer-based program. Their cooperation would be crucial at such stages as job design and the recruitment, training, and supervision of volunteers. A volunteer coordinator's task is to enlist the enthusiastic participation of paid staff so that they will perceive volunteers as an important program resource. The facilitating nature of this task requires that a coordinator hold formal and informal meetings with paid staff and volunteers, and especially that he or she provides for the efficient flow of information. Any failure to involve paid staff in a volunteer-based program might cause them to develop fears or misunderstandings concerning their own jobs, which could affect a program adversely.

Job Design

Job design (discussed in detail in Chapter 5) means writing job descriptions that clearly state the responsibilities, obligations, powers, and privileges of particular roles. The advantages are (1) a person can make a more intelligent decision about becoming a volunteer than if no job description was available; (2) early job design lends structure to a program and leads to the planning of such activities as recruitment, supervision, and evaluation of volunteers; and (3) if needed, roles can be altered and job descriptions changed to coincide with changes in the organization.

RECRUITMENT AND SELECTION OF VOLUNTEERS

Recruitment and selection of volunteers actually begins with the established criteria of job descriptions. The careful writing of job descriptions should clearly delineate the responsibilities of volunteers and thus suggest the criteria to be used in selecting them. Usually a volunteer coordinator, in consultation with paid staff and other program personnel, determines the criteria. For example, one criterion for selecting volunteers to work with senior citizens might be prior experience. The recruitment of such volunteers gains focus when based on a job description.

Recruitment

The next step entails active recruitment of potential volunteers according to the criteria established. Questions to be addressed include these: Who will do the recruiting? What methods and techniques, including the use of media, will be employed? Where will volunteers be sought? Can community resources offer any help? Usually a volunteer coordinator heads a recruitment drive, in which he or she plays the role of an educator, dispensing information to volunteer candidates about their prospective duties and to an organization about the progress of the drive. A more complete analysis of the recruitment process appears in Chapter 5.

Application Design and Interview

The selection process is a winnowing activity in which the volunteer coordinator seeks, on the basis of the established criteria, candidates who appear well suited to the particular volunteer roles. Commonly, he or she designs application forms and arranges interviews based on the information submitted. Ideally, an interview is a shared experience in which a volunteer coordinator, perhaps in conjunction with a paid official of the organization, examines a candidate's potential as a volunteer and the candidate tries to assess the value of the proposed experience. Detailed guidelines for interviewing volunteers appear in Chapter 6.

The Selection Agreement

After information gained from the application form and the interview has been processed, decisions are made on whether or not to enlist the services of a volunteer. Once an affirmative decision has been reached, a formal agreement is drawn up between the organization and the volunteer. This agreement (described more fully in Chapter 6) is intended not merely to seal the arrangement but to outline expectations. It might contain such items as a volunteer's responsibilities and privileges, scheduling of his or her time, location of assignments, and meeting dates. As one of his or her main responsibilities, the task of a volunteer coordinator is to reach agreement on these points while establishing a foundation of mutual understanding.

SOCIALIZATION AND TRAINING

The socialization and training aspects of a volunteer-based program are envisaged as taking place during the initial phase of a volunteer's experience, but they can continue throughout the program. Some activities that can help to equip volunteers with the skills, knowledge, or attitudes necessary for the efficient performance of their jobs include orientation and preservice training programs, all of which should be conducted prior to placement of volunteers. In-service training provides additional learning experiences once volunteers have become adjusted to their working situations. Further coverage of these activities is offered in Chapter 6.

To adequately train and socialize volunteers, a volunteer coordinator assumes the role of a facilitator who seeks the particular blend of subject matter and methods which will lead to optimum learning experiences within the limits of available resources. In some instances, he or she will have to don the mantle of an instructor who actually delivers the subject matter, become a media specialist, or assume the role of a diagnostician.

Orientation

The main purpose of orientation is to help volunteers become acquainted with others in the program, to learn the ways of an organization and the goals of a volunteer-based program, and to comprehend their own roles in it. Manuals frequently prepared for this purpose might contain a background statement about a program, the rules and regulations of an organization, tips on maximizing the volunteer experience, and other information designed to help volunteers become adjusted to new situations. Sometimes, a volunteer coordinator handles orientation in a personalized manner, arranging one-to-one conversations. Otherwise, orientation occurs in a group situation which offers opportunities for volunteers to share concerns or ask pertinent questions. One outcome of a well-conducted orientation period will be a climate of mutual understanding and acceptance by all parties concerned with the volunteer-based program.

Preservice Training

Often, preservice training involves a volunteer coordinator in preassessment of volunteers' capabilities, careful instruction, and evaluation of their learning. The purpose is to equip volunteers with the skills needed to perform job responsibilities. Such training becomes less arduous in cases where volunteers have had prior experience in the duties they are to assume—for example, clerical work, child care, and proposal writing. However, when the subject matter is specialized and the volunteers are to assume technical responsibilities, as in a museum, zoo, or public aquarium setting, a consultant usually conducts the training. When the content is to include the history, policies, and regulations of an organization, a volunteer coordinator confronts a choice. Either he or she conducts the session, participates as a member of the team, or delegates responsibility.

Placement

Placement occurs when it has been determined that a volunteer possesses the proficiencies needed to undertake certain responsibilities and when he or she appears comfortable in a situation. In some cases volunteers will be fully qualified to be placed immediately. In other cases volunteers will not be fully prepared for the task at hand and will require some form of training. Placement, therefore, follows orientation and preservice training in this discussion. Where a job represents a new or difficult learning experience for a volunteer, a coordinator will need to make careful observations and even to ponder changing an assignment when the volunteer does not fit the task. Often it is assumed that changing a volunteer's role is inappropriate. It is not unusual for several changes in placement to be made, such as when a volunteer's desires and capabilities do not match the requirements of the job. Thus, a volunteer coordinator must be prepared to greet a variety of situations in the placement of volunteers.

In-Service Training

After accumulating experience in a work situation, a volunteer often becomes aware of a need to gain additional skills or to refine existing ones. (The varied methods and techniques available for this purpose are outlined in Chapter 6.) Before employing any of them, a coordinator should carefully diagnose the individual learning needs of each volunteer and select the appropriate content areas and instructional processes that will lead to a rich learning experience.

GUIDANCE

The demands placed on volunteers to enter new situations, meet new people, and practice new skills can be overwhelming. It is the task of a coordinator to analyze difficulties in adjustment, including personal problems which might impede performance, and to reduce anxiety. The goal is to enhance the motivation of volunteers and increase their satisfaction, while improving the productivity of the program.

Motivation

A coordinator who wishes to build motivation must understand the personal goals of individual volunteers and check regularly to ensure that these goals are being fulfilled. If not, a coordinator might expand a job to make it more challenging, reassign jobs, or suggest new learning experiences that will give a volunteer a sense of renewal.

Supervision

The process of supervision will yield insights to a coordinator about the morale of volunteers. Hence, in overseeing their activities, he or she will scrutinize not only their productivity but also such factors as attendance, punctuality, and personal relationships for indications of the state of morale. A basic requirement is that a coordinator must be prepared to make an honest appraisal of a volunteer's strengths and weaknesses, to discuss them candidly with a volunteer, and to suggest constructive ways to improve performance.

Recognition

In extending formal recognition to volunteers, a coordinator might arrange dinners and luncheons, or make awards in the form of certificates and letters of appreciation. The keynote is sincerity, which can be aided by specific mention of a volunteer's contribution, as opposed to a general expression of appreciation. (The topic of recognition is discussed further in Chapter 7.)

ADMINISTRATION

The purpose of so-called administrative activities is to facilitate a productive working environment which produces mutual benefits for the program and the volunteer. The major difference between administrative activities and those grouped under "Guidance" resides in the nature of the activities. Those directly concerned with the management and well-being of volunteers, such as motivation and recognition, are guidance activities. Those activities which do not directly affect volunteers, such as management of the office (including record keeping and proposal writing), establishment of community linkages, and maintenance activities are considered to be administrative activities. Though indirect, administrative activities give way to a particular climate for volunteer participation—one that often depends on the style of the administrator.

Management

Although many office responsibilities can be delegated, a coordinator is frequently accountable for results. Examples of responsibilities in this category are record-keeping systems, progress reports to organization decision makers, dissemination of information to paid staff and volunteers and, possibly, fiscal planning, alertness to new sources of funds, and clerical duties. (Detailed discussion of these responsibilities appears in Chapter 7.)

Evaluation

As indicated in Chapter 8, evaluation is a multistage plan used by a coordinator, outside experts, or paid staff, among others, to analyze various aspects of a volunteer-based program with a view to improving it. The purpose of a particular evaluation study might vary from upgrading certain aspects of a program to deciding whether to adopt an innovation.

Linkage Development

Linkages between a volunteer-based program and certain community organizations and agencies make possible a sharing of resources, especially when those groups avow similar purposes. Potential areas of cooperation include joint recruitment campaigns, shared public relations, common training programs, and endeavors toward the cooperative acquisition of materials. An astute coordinator will recognize that such shared activities not only hold out the hope of cost savings but might actually broaden the scope of a program.

Continuing Education of a Volunteer Coordinator

Finding and taking advantage of opportunities for further learning and/or personal growth can reasonably be considered an aspect of the role of a coordinator. He or she can plan well in advance to attend conferences, workshops, and meetings that deal with relevant topics, to undertake course work, to visit other programs, and to pursue independent study.

Until recently, few educational opportunities have existed for volunteer coordinators in adult education—opportunities to share ideas, invent standards of success, or shape the creative side of the role. But, with the surge of interest in voluntarism, new opportunities are emerging. Coalitions and associations have been formed, such as the Association for Administration of Volunteer Services, Association of Voluntary Action Scholars, Alliance for Volunteerism and, Volunteer (National Center for Citizen Involvement). These groups are composed of practitioners, scholars, and volunteers working toward the creation of models of organizational management relating to volunteers. These models will become increasingly useful as the movement gains momentum. In addition, there is an increase in the number of workshops, institutes, and roundtable meetings on voluntarism, with attention to such topics as grantsmanship, self-awareness, evaluation, conducting workshops, legal training, staff-volunteer relations, fund raising, and supervision techniques. As for the universities, they are offering degree programs in the administration of volunteer-based programs. Clearly, the intent is to furnish practitioners with insights and competencies related to the social and political sciences and to deal with issues that pertain specifically to voluntarism. A university course of study usually blends theory, research, and practice to produce a kind of vision of voluntarism. The multidisciplinary nature of a master's or bachelor's program can be judged from its content areas: organizational theory, management studies, the volunteer organization, American studies, statistics, managerial accounting, marketing, social change, communications, politics, futurism, and psychology.

CONCLUSION

This chapter began with a hypothetical announcement of a vacant position for a volunteer coordinator and proceeded to develop various aspects of that role. It has become apparent that the role is much more complex than it seems—so much so that an organization which contemplates hiring a coordinator might feel compelled to develop selective criteria based on the responsibilities outlined in this chapter. As for a coordinator, he or she should find comfort in the knowledge that a growing number of agencies and institutions offer assistance in various ways.

Two interrelated themes emerge from the above discussion. One is that the establishment and sequencing of program activities define the responsibilities and hence shape the role of a volunteer coordinator. Another is that the fluid and extensive nature of that role, in turn, affects operation of the program. The conclusion must be that neither organizational structure nor leadership alone is sufficient to ensure the success of a program.

The role of a coordinator requires the creative management of people, resources, and opportunities—that is, an ability to inspire people to develop their highest potential and a propensity to discover, even create opportunities. To be creative, then, is to be proactive (not merely reactive), to devise alternatives (not merely perceive them), and to strive to shape the future (not merely plan it). According to Peter Drucker, an important characteristic of an effective leader is that he or she has a focus on the future, an "outward contribution," as opposed to an orientation to the past.[1]

[1]Peter Drucker, *The Effective Executive,* Harper and Row, New York, 1967, p. 24.

Chapter 4

The Importance of Climates for Volunteer Participation: An Examination of Varying Types

INTRODUCTION

As discussed in previous chapters, building and maintaining a productive volunteer-based program involves more than coordinating program activities. An additional consideration, which is fundamental to the process, is creating an optimum climate for volunteer participation. By "climate" is meant a predominant set of standards, attitudes, and conditions that govern a volunteer-based program. An ideal climate is one which results in satisfaction of the needs of both the volunteers and the organization. Also, a climate

> . . . should be one which causes adults to feel accepted, respected, and supported; in which there is freedom of expression without fear of punishment or ridicule.[1]

[1]Malcolm S. Knowles, *The Modern Practice of Adult Education: Andragogy versus Pedagogy,* Association Press, New York, 1973, p. 41.

To create a positive climate for volunteer participation means being mindful of the needs of volunteers, as well as striving to accomplish the goals and objectives of the organization.

The purpose of this chapter is to investigate a range of working climates which permits, as far as possible, the integration of volunteers' needs and organizational demands. We will explore three commonly held managerial beliefs or attitudes about volunteers, each of which underlies a distinct type of program. This discussion will be followed by a continuum of corresponding climates.

THREE MANAGERIAL BELIEFS ABOUT VOLUNTEERS

Every administrator, manager, or coordinator entertains beliefs about the nature of people in general and of subordinates in particular. These beliefs are certain to be reflected in the leadership style chosen, which has implications for the way decisions are made and the nature of interpersonal relations. Frequently, the success of a volunteer coordinater is linked directly to the consistency of his or her attitudes about and toward volunteers, attitudes that markedly affect the conduct of a program. The three managerial beliefs to be investigated are called the "calculative volunteer," "participatory volunteer," and "self-actualizing volunteer."[2]

The Calculative Volunteer

Douglas McGregor asserts that beliefs about human nature influence managerial style. His model, referred to as theory X and theory Y, dichotomizes two managerial approaches which can be extended to the volunteer setting.[3] Theory X assumes that organizational goals can best be reached when workers are tightly controlled through specific task instructions and strict supervision. The theory leans toward a mechanistic style of management. By contrast, theory Y assumes that organizational goals are reached more readily when workers are highly motivated, are given decision-making responsibilities, and can share in the overall success of the organization. Theory Y is interpreted as a participational or humanistic approach to management.

Coordinators who assume volunteers to be calculative adopt a philosophy that resembles theory X. Specifically, the assumptions may include the following:

[2]Terms adapted from Edgar Schien, *Organizational Psychology,* Prentice-Hall, Englewood Cliffs, N.J., 1965, pp. 47–63.
[3]Douglas McGregor, *The Human Side of Enterprise,* McGraw-Hill, New York, 1960, pp. 34–35.

1   People volunteer for their own purposes and gains.
2   Volunteers are unreliable and require, even prefer, being controlled by the organizational management.
3   Volunteers avoid organizational responsibility since others, not they, are paid to make decisions.
4   Volunteers' goals are opposed to those of the organization.
5   Volunteers are incapable of self-discipline and self-control because of their irrational feelings.

The corresponding management style stresses the establishment of strict lines of authority, clearly defined responsibilities, and well-planned goals and objectives. Volunteers are rarely offered decision-making responsibilities, nor are their opinions considered necessary in shaping the program. Rather, volunteers are regarded as a means toward an end, a factor of production, in meeting the expressed objectives of the organization. Therefore, the burden of success rests with management.

The Participatory Volunteer

McGregor's theory Y depicts workers as self-motivated and interested in the job, with a capacity to be creative and to assume responsibility. Hence, they are motivated by a need to participate and share in the decision-making process. To adapt this view to a volunteer setting, the coordinator who believes that volunteers are participatory by nature probably makes the following assumptions:

1   Volunteers find a sense of identity through contact with others.
2   The act of volunteering offers a way to initiate friendships and to gain a sense of purpose.
3   Volunteers will respond to the instructions of a volunteer coordinator if an adequate social setting is provided.
4   Volunteers are responsive to their peer group and seek to form cohesive group relations.

These assumptions dictate that a given program will be volunteer-centered, not organization-centered. The implications for management follow accordingly: to be attentive to the needs of volunteers, their feelings of acceptance, and the social setting; to worry less about commanding the obedience of volunteers and, instead, to encourage group initiative and teamwork. In this situation, coordinators become facilitators and supporters as well as buffers to the challenges and mandates from high-level decision makers. One aspect of this philosophy is that if the social factors affecting the group are "right"—that is, if volunteers feel themselves a part of the program, sharers in decisions—turnover will be low because volunteers are likely to remain with the program. Under these circumstances, the burden rests on management to facilitate agreement between volunteers and the organization, with emphasis on team building and group decision making.

The Self-Actualizing Volunteer

Abraham Maslow defines self-actualization as a higher-order human need which acts as a motivator for many people. Specifically, this need involves a process of growth which leads one toward the " . . . complete development and fruition of one's resources and potentialities and consequent feeling of growth, maturity, health, and autonomy."[4] Self-actualization can motivate people only when the basic physiological, safety, love and affection, and esteem needs have all been satisfied.[5] If the environmental conditions are conducive and a person is motivated to make full use of his or her capacities, then it can be said that he or she is becoming self-actualized. A volunteer coordinator who believes that people are motivated by the self-actualizing need regard the volunteer as one who requires meaning from volunteer experiences.

The volunteer coordinator must display a management style which considers relationships among tasks to be accomplished, the structure of the organization, and the characteristics of the personnel.

The accompanying assumptions about volunteers include the following:

1　Volunteers wish to be responsible and can be self-directed.

2　Responsibility involves having an adequate time perspective, the needed skills and abilities, and an understanding of the organization's goals and objectives.

3　Volunteers have a clear sense of self-improvement that seeks to understand and correct their own shortcomings.

4　External controls will be looked upon as a threat to the volunteer.

5　Social situations cannot be mandated or controlled, but must evolve and grow naturally.

6　Volunteers will willingly adapt to the structure of the organization and accept its philosophy and goals.

The implications for management are similar to those that apply to the participatory volunteer in the sense that the work the volunteers do needs to be meaningful and rewarding. The chief difference lies in the degree of control assumed by the volunteer. That is, self-actualizing volunteers are generally more able to assume responsibility and hence tend to be better self-starters than participatory volunteers. The managerial

---

[4] Abraham Maslow, *Motivation and Personality*, Harper and Row, New York, 1970, p. 69.

[5] Ibid., p. 91.

goal is not so much to fulfill social needs but to help the self-actualizing volunteer reach his or her self-potential through volunteer experiences. Hence, proper recognition, honesty, open criticism, and trust become important managerial actions. If volunteers learn, grow, and enjoy new experiences in a volunteer setting, they are likely to remain faithful to the job and to become avid supporters of a program.

In this situation, a coordinator becomes less of an authority figure and more of a facilitator or counselor. The "authority" to get the job done is invested in the role of the volunteer. Volunteers are expected to respond to the challenge of the assignment. The organization is expected to provide the necessary guidance, instruction, and evaluation. Volunteers gain a satisfaction that is intrinsic to the challenge. The organization gains the expertise and dedication of volunteers. This relationship may cause volunteers to internalize the norms of the organization and develop a moral commitment to it. If belief in the work is strong, great potential will be released.

Thus far we have considered three singular managerial assumptions about volunteers. Each assumption rests on a belief of what motivates volunteers. The calculative volunteer is motivated by expected extrinsic rewards, the participatory volunteer by social needs, and the self-actualizing volunteer by intrinsic rewards, or personal growth. It must be remembered that volunteers are individuals, each with complex needs and motives that are liable to change according to the situation in which they find themselves. Furthermore, in time, volunteers might exhibit new motives and set new goals. We can conclude that volunteers will react differently to different management styles, and that it is the responsibility of the volunteer coordinator to recognize the type of leadership that offers the greatest benefit to the volunteers and to the organization.

A CONTINUUM OF WORKING CLIMATES

As mentioned earlier, managerial assumptions about volunteers may be a determining factor in the type of working climate that emerges. In comparing two of the three managerial beliefs stated above, the climate typically created for the calculative volunteer contrasts sharply with that created for the participatory volunteer. In the former, organizational efficiency and productivity tend to be emphasized, often at the expense of social, informal aspects of a program. The latter is seen as minimizing the goal attainment and productivity of an organization and maximizing satisfaction of the expressed social needs of volunteers. The ideal climate for the self-actualizing volunteer places emphasis on personal growth. Yet, the ideal is not always attainable. For example, in some emergency lifesaving programs, the sense of urgency precludes compromise on the part of an organization to fit the needs of the volunteers. In other organiza-

	Selected program activities		
Types of climates	Socialization	Training	Guidance
Open	H	H	H
Autonomous	H	H	M
Controlled	L	H	H
Familiar	H	L	L
Paternalistic	L	L	M
Closed	L	L	L

Figure 4-1   H-high emphasis; M-medium emphasis; L-low emphasis.

tions, it would be easier to provide for socialization, to individualize training, and to guide volunteers toward their particular goals. A coordinator cannot guarantee either organizational productivity or the gratification of volunteers' social needs. However, a realization of the range of possible climates is important because it helps in understanding managerial options.

In an analysis of seventy-one educational institutions, Andrew Halpin and Donald Croft observed six different kinds of climates, based upon such factors as leadership style, morale, and intimacy among staff.[6] This research, which was performed in public schools (where volunteers have been used extensively as support staff) is relevant to volunteer-based programs because it establishes a relationship between leadership style and type of climate. Halpin's model is applicable to many types of adult education agencies. The types of indicators used to distinguish climates can also be used to differentiate volunteer programs as well, such as the existence and power of a hierarchy, adherence to job descriptions, leadership style, use of rules and regulations, and morale. The resulting continuum of types of climates characterizes the opposite ends as "open" and "closed," according to organizational flexibility or rigidity. Between the extremes lie the "autonomous," "controlled," "familiar," and "paternalistic" climates. Each of the six climates shows a different combination of such indicators.

An attempt will be made to differentiate six climates, using practical indicators such as socialization (emphasis on the process by which volunteers are introduced to a group setting), training (emphasis on providing skills to volunteers), and guidance (emphasis on providing leadership and a sense of direction to volunteers and attending to their personal growth). Figure 4-1 shows the six climates and describes them according to the emphasis given to socialization, training, and guidance.

[6]Andrew W. Halpin and Donald B. Croft, *Organizational Climate of Schools,* Midwest Administrative Center, University of Chicago, Chicago, 1963.

An Open Climate

An open climate demonstrates a balance between meeting volunteers' social needs and maintaining high standards of efficiency. Success in achieving this balance depends heavily upon the ability of a volunteer coordinator to establish a democratic decision-making process and a two-way communication flow. He or she must provide encouragement and support when morale declines and utilize controls to enforce standards when productivity falters. However, because morale is usually high, productivity seldom has to be stressed. Typically, a leader shows trust and compassion toward volunteers and frequently delegates responsibility to them. Such exemplary behavior earns the respect of volunteers.

The socialization process reflects an awareness of the needs, motives, and goals of volunteers. New volunteers experience a high degree of acceptance by the group and sense cohesiveness among its members. At orientation sessions, they receive information about the history and goals of an organization and about the mission of a volunteer-based program. Once new volunteers have become acculturated to an organization and understand the values and standards of a program, they are encouraged to interact and to participate in planning and decision-making processes. The strengths and weaknesses of new volunteers are noted by a volunteer coordinator so that he or she can design appropriate staff development programs for them.

Although rules and regulations exist, they are not forced upon volunteers. Instead, efforts are made to have their purposes understood so that volunteers will comply willingly. Routine work is handled in much the same way. Generally, decisions about how routine work is to be accomplished are left to volunteers, who develop a sense of pride in their work as they manage the business day in a democratic way.

In an open climate, the hierarchy of an organization is understood and not questioned. Hence, volunteers do not threaten the status of paid staff and it becomes easy to form friendly relationships and promote a warm atmosphere among paid and nonpaid personnel. Among volunteers there is adherence to rules and responsibilities outlined in the job description, yet job rotation occurs, enabling them to experience new learning situations.

Training is valued by volunteers who display a motivation to learn. Opportunities for learning appear in the form of seminars, workshops, and courses. Training programs are periodically evaluated to keep them pertinent, a process aided by the willingness of volunteers to provide input about the utility of subject matter. In this way and others, volunteers can determine the direction of their learning. Occasionally, funds are sought to reimburse volunteers for tuition costs or registration fees.

An open climate provides guidance for volunteers as well as opportunities for them to assess their short- and long-range goals in consultation with a coordinator. If volunteers are dissatisfied with assigned work, adjustments are made. Recognizing individual difference, a volunteer coordinator avoids placing undue emphasis on conformity. Where volunteers feel a need for additional opportunities, new goals can be established and new learning opportunities created. Volunteers receive an honest appraisal of their own strengths and weaknesses, and are encouraged to make an honest appraisal of a program. If problems surface, a volunteer coordinator is prepared to offer assistance. Rarely does he or she indulge in scolding or ridicule. Rather, the role resembles that of diagnostician. By being realistic about observed behavior a volunteer coordinator can be of tremendous help to volunteers, especially in areas of difficulty. Recognition of volunteers is a motivator as well. It takes the form of reminding them of their contributions to a program, and showing gratitude for their efforts.

To summarize, an open climate is marked by high morale, high participation, and shared decision making. The values and attitudes of volunteers agree with program goals, and the leadership style reflects attention to organizational goals and compassion for volunteers.

An Autonomous Climate

According to Halpin, the autonomous climate also emphasizes high morale for volunteers, though somewhat less than does the open climate. The chief difference is that a leader chooses to remain more aloof from the staff. This is not to say that there is resistance to expressive or informal activities. As long as productivity is high, volunteers will be responsible for satisfying their own social needs. The result is an effective democratic decision-making process and a sense of pride arising from group involvement. Efficiency does not have to be stressed for, as in the open climate, there is an apparent motivation to comply. The communication pattern suggests a high emphasis on upward communication and medium emphasis on downward communication; that is, the coordinator listens to the concerns of the volunteers, but does not share the concerns of the program or issue orders. In other words, volunteers are encouraged to voice their concerns, with assurance that they will be listened to.

Socialization is regarded as a strength of the autonomous climate. The group works well together, especially when engaged in activities related to task achievement. New volunteers find a spirit of acceptance and are swiftly brought into the process, sometimes by a volunteer coordinator but more often by veteran volunteers. On their efforts hinges the success or failure of this acculturation process. The group then becomes a source of satisfaction for volunteers, because of its effectiveness in accomplishing assigned tasks and for its gratification of social needs.

The hierarchy and functions of the organization are understood and not questioned by volunteers. Although little emphasis is paid to the formulation of working relationships with paid staff, volunteers are generally regarded as assets to the organization. A warm and functional relationship exists among the volunteer group. Rotation of assignments occurs infrequently. Although volunteers are generally able to manage without a coordinator, they treat one with respect and assent to the few demands he or she places on them. Volunteers may recognize that a volunteer coordinator faces other heavy demands and respect the resulting time constraints.

Training is important to both a volunteer coordinator and the volunteers, but there is no long-range training program and meetings or workshops are of a pragmatic nature. Volunteers suggest training ideas to a volunteer coordinator, who is responsible for providing or facilitating the training. Therefore, training becomes largely a short-range activity.

In the autonomous climate, there would be little guidance if it were not for the support given by the group itself. A volunteer coordinator, although considerate and attentive, does not view guidance as a high priority and ignores problems relating to job satisfaction and those brought to the group's attention. Often the group itself is able to find effective solutions. However, little systematic assessment goes on, either by the group or by the volunteer coordinator. Only when problems become urgent are they submitted to the group.

The autonomous climate features an aloof, yet considerate and possbily overcommitted volunteer coordinator who allows volunteers to attend to many details and decisions of the program. The group is usually effective at achieving organizational ends, although the priority lies in the camaraderie of its members. Consequently, morale and participation are high.

A Controlled Climate

A controlled climate denotes a neutral level of morale (either high or low), considerable emphasis on efficiency, and relatively little emphasis on gratification of volunteers' social needs. Volunteers are encouraged to produce results rather than engage in expressive activities. The leadership style reflects this attitude, coupled with an unwillingness to share authority. A volunteer coordinator is task-oriented, interested in building a rigid organizational structure. Consequently, great emphasis is given to downward communication, especially in the form of orders, but slight emphasis is paid to upward communication or listening to volunteers' concerns. Organizational ends are systematically pursued, and the achievement of those ends produces some gratification to volunteers.

Socialization is routinized, projecting the desire that volunteers understand precisely what is required of them. A volunteer coordinator takes charge and explains the limits of responsibility to new volunteers. The amount of information needed to accomplish a task is offered to the volunteers prior to placement. Little attention is paid to group cohesiveness, but great attention is paid to task accomplishment. Volunteers are encouraged to perform effectively, and receive information about the required routine work and the processes of training and evaluation.

Compliance with rules and regulations is deemed necessary and is enforced. Perhaps the basic rule is that volunteers must obey a volunteer coordinator, who is responsible for achieving high production. Volunteers are also expected to understand the hierarchy of the organization and to remain within the limits of job descriptions which discourage the establishment of relations with paid staff. Rarely does job rotation occur. The predominant concern is that the job gets done.

The training offered to volunteers is designed to fit job descriptions, and attendance is mandatory. The objectives of training are to increase job performance, rather than to foster volunteers' personal growth. So, the workshops and meetings are likely to be structured and self-contained, offering little opportunity to volunteers to shape the direction of their learning.

Guidance is a priority, not because of a volunteer coordinator's concern for volunteers but because of a desire to achieve organizational goals. Volunteers are held tightly to job descriptions, and any variance is quickly detected and remedied by a volunteer coordinator. Evaluation of volunteer performance is frequent. If a volunteer expresses dissatisfaction with the work, the response is to terminate his or her service.

The controlled climate allows little room for volunteers to express their concerns or to share in the planning of an organization's functions. These are strictly controlled by a volunteer coordinator.

A Familiar Climate

Whereas a controlled climate is distinguished by an emphasis on efficiency and neglect of social concerns, a familiar climate is known for stressing social concerns and downplaying efficiency. The subsequent leadership style stresses social concerns. Few rules exist, because rules are seen as impairing the social dimension. Consequently, business affairs are taken care of in chaotic fashion. Volunteers gain a sense of satisfaction from belonging, not from goal achievement. Hence, morale is at a neutral level and little emphasis is placed on downward communication. A volunteer coordinator does not motivate volunteers toward productivity. Upward communication is emphasized, however, because the volunteer coordinator is attentive to their expressed needs.

The goal of the socialization process is to accommodate volunteers to the social setting and to instill a "friendly" group spirit. New volunteers are readily accepted into the group and are made to feel at ease. Socialization is not handled the same way for every volunteer, due to an inclination toward the forming of personal relationships. Briefings and explanations of organizational policies and procedures are minimized.

A volunteer coordinator does not burden volunteers with routine work, but takes care of it alone, believing that this course of action will avert conflict or resentment. Rules and regulations are practically nonexistent, being perceived by a volunteer coordinator as a threat to morale.

The hierarchy of an organization is not explained, and little attempt is made to form functional relationships with paid staff, although such events can occur. Some organization members regard volunteers as unnecessary, a view that is resisted by a volunteer coordinator. Volunteers manifest a casual attitude because lines of authority are nonexistent. Although volunteers acknowledge that a volunteer coordinator is sincere in his or her efforts to provide a friendly social setting, they lack motivation toward production.

Training to equip volunteers with the skills to do a job is not a priority. Instead, meetings tend to resemble social experiences designed to bolster morale. Occasionally, volunteers seek training elsewhere.

Guidance, in the sense of help offered to volunteers in reaching short- and long-range goals, is minimized because of the lack of concern for organizational goals. Rather, there is concern for volunteers' well-being, expressed in attention to such problems as transportation, child care, and recognition of accomplishments. A volunteer coordinator does not believe that criticizing volunteers is productive and strives, instead, to form close relationships. Recognition is viewed as an important function.

A familiar climate is characterized by a disregard for organizational goals and high regard for volunteers' social needs. A leader tries hard to please volunteers, but assumes no responsibility for their growth or productivity. Morale is neutral because volunteers tend to enjoy the social situation but gain little satisfaction from task achievement.

A Paternalistic Climate

A paternalistic climate is exemplified by high conflict among staff, factionalism, an overbearing leader, and low morale. While opportunity exists for gratification of social needs, it usually fails to occur due to the leader's inability to share responsibilities, provide guidance, or foster a friendly spirit. In fact, it appears to volunteers that a volunteer coordinator distrusts and resents them, yet it is evident that he or she has invested much time and energy in the running of the volunteer-based program. Neither goal achievement nor social needs are realized. The resulting communication pattern shows considerable, yet ineffective emphasis on the downward pattern and slight emphasis on the upward.

Usually a leader is not interested in the social concerns of volunteers or in instilling a sense of efficiency. New volunteers are introduced to others in the hope that they will take responsibility for answering questions and helping newcomers become acquainted with other people and the ways of the program. However, due to the low morale of veteran volunteers, new ones primarily learn about problems and conflicts. Sometimes cliques are formed when veteran volunteers are unwilling to accept new volunteers and view them as a threat.

There is much routine work, which is grudgingly undertaken by volunteers, but little emphasis on rules and regulations. A volunteer coordinator tries to make the experience as pleasant as possible for volunteers. But with little productive spirit, they become apathetic toward the organization and the busy work given them. Avoiding responsibility, chronic absenteeism, and high turnover become commonplace.

The hierarchy of the organization is not fully understood by the volunteers, and the purpose of a volunteer-based program is not understood by paid staff. Even though a volunteer coordinator attempts to thwart criticism by paid staff, volunteers are nevertheless regarded as a hindrance. Conflicts which arise between the two groups often require a volunteer coordinator's intervention.

Training volunteers is neither encouraged nor discouraged, but few opportunities for training exist. The occasional meetings are poorly attended and characterized by debate and argument. When a leader attempts to resolve a conflict, he or she is often seen as an intruder.

A volunteer coordinator attempts to learn about the problems of volunteers, but guidance is, on the whole, very directive. However, the actions he or she takes often do not help volunteers overcome their problems.

A paternalistic climate is marked by low morale and a sense of factionalism. Some interaction occurs and some guidance is offered, but not enough to raise the low morale. A leader is not attentive to the needs of volunteers, except when one wishes to drop out or when outside criticism forces action. In these matters, a volunteer coordinator is largely ineffective.

A Closed Climate

A closed climate is similar to a paternalistic one, as shown by the shared characterisitics of low morale and failure to achieve organizational goals or to satisfy volunteers' social needs. The difference lies in the businesslike nature of a leader and his or her failure to provide any kind of social activity or guidance for volunteers. In this climate, a leader shows no consideration for volunteers. Consequently, there is high turnover among them and activities tend to be temporary in nature. Both upward and downward patterns of communication are negative.

Socialization is nonexistent. Volunteers are expected to perform their duties without acculturation or social interaction. There is no regard for their needs, nor is any attempt made to make them proud of the organization. Generally, volunteers are expected to perform their duties in isolation, unaware of the effects of their efforts. Morale is understandably low and apathy high.

Rules and regulations are usually nonexistent or temporary, but routine detail work is abundant. A volunteer alone decides whether to perform a menial task, and usually decides against it. A leader does not enforce rules and tolerates low efficiency.

No attempt is made to explain the hierarchy of either the organization or the volunteer-based program. Volunteers are frequently criticized by paid staff, but a volunteer coordinator does not respond. No one, including volunteers, is quite certain what they are supposed to do.

In this climate opportunities for training are unavailable, nor are meetings held for volunteers. Should the issue of training arise, it usually comes totally from volunteers. Training is not viewed as beneficial. The guidance factor is also low, meaning that the social needs, problems, short- and long-range goals, and recognition of volunteers are neglected.

A closed climate is characterized by an absence of effective leadership, few opportunities for volunteers, and low morale. No concern is shown for volunteer participation in helping to shape productivity or for the satisfaction of social needs. Consequently, turnover is high and little is accomplished.

CONCLUSION

One purpose of this chapter is to point out that certain climates are more conducive to volunteer participation than others. Inasmuch as a mutually beneficial arrangement between an organization and a volunteer is the aim, the assertion can be made that the open and autonomous climates are more desirable than those paternalistic and closed ones. This assertion is based on the conviction that volunteers are more often self-actualizing and participatory than calculative. When warranted, volunteers can and do accept responsibility. With proper socialization, training, and guidance, volunteers are quite capable of self-discipline and rational productive activity.

Without attempting any precise comparisons, it is possible to detect how attitudes and assumptions concerning volunteers can affect a working climate. For example, the self-actualizing volunteer roughly corresponds to the autonomous climate, the participatory volunteer to the controlled or familiar climate, and the calculative volunteer to the paternalistic or closed climate. The combination of the self-actualizing volunteer and the participatory volunteer seems to produce the open climate. In short, the creation of a climate for volunteer participation begins with managerial beliefs about volunteers.

Another purpose of presenting descriptions of climates is to demonstrate how different climates influence program activities. It is hoped that such discussion will lead to informed choices among the types of climate and activities appropriate to different volunteer settings. Depending on the type of volunteer organization, a different emphasis will no doubt be placed on such factors as socialization, training, guidance, and communication. Although the climates are presented as though they were discrete, it is possible to establish a combination of climates.

As for controlling the three program activities presented in Figure 4-1—socialization, training, and guidance—reasoned approaches can be taken which may lead an organization toward a certain climate. In the case of these three activities, concrete preplanning can help ensure a favorable climate. Owing to the large amount of attention paid to these activities elsewhere in the book, a lengthy discussion of varying types of socialization, training, and guidance need not occur here. It is enough to realize the dynamics of the relationship between the program emphasis afforded them and the resultant climate.

The open climate, deemed appropriate for most volunteer-based programs, results from (or perhaps causes) strong emphasis on each of the three program activities. By way of stark contrast, the closed climate is marked by complete neglect of such activities. In other words, the conspicuous omission of concern for the socialization, training, and guidance of volunteers directs a program toward a closed climate. Viewed this way, a closed climate is not achieved but results from an absence of concern for volunteer participation. An open climate is achieved through an abundance of concern for voluntary participation and careful preplanning.

Chapter 5

Recruitment of Volunteers

INTRODUCTION

Recently, when an urban-based adult literacy program came into existence, one of the first decisions made by the neophyte coordinator was to recruit volunteers as tutors. Subsequently, a recruitment campaign was launched. Flyers and brochures were prepared and distributed, advertisements appeared in local newspapers, and speeches and interviews were arranged with community-based service organizations and representatives of the local radio station. As a result of this campaign, thirty people committed themselves as volunteers. However, shortly thereafter, volunteers began dropping out until only seven remained after 6 weeks.

What went wrong? Was this decline normal? Were the volunteers the wrong kind of people? Who or what was at fault? In this case, the problem lay with the volunteer coordinator's lack of knowledge of how to proceed—specifically his failure to realize that recruitment is not an isolated activity but is closely related to and follows such activities as job design, development of selection criteria, and establishment of training requirements. Job design involves writing job descriptions that clearly reveal the tasks to be performed by volunteers; selection criteria represent an attempt to "match" volunteers to tasks; and training requirements provide the knowledge, skills, and attitudes needed to perform the tasks. Other factors which the coordinator may have disregarded include systematic determination of the number of volunteers needed and knowledge of why people volunteer. In short, he did not realize that recruitment is a process and that without structure it is doomed to failure.

A key feature of the recruitment process is the imparting of information about a volunteer-based program to rouse people's interest and ultimately persuade them to volunteer. The major purpose of this chapter is to explore selected elements of the recruitment process: determining roles and analyzing tasks, writing job descriptions, investigating potential sources of volunteers, and selecting a promotional plan.

DETERMINING ROLES AND ANALYZING TASKS

It would be exceedingly difficult to exhaust all possibilities for volunteer involvement in adult education. The eventual determination of roles in a particular organization hinges on the capacity of the program to support new roles and/or to expand its goals on the basis of organizational needs. The following list of volunteer roles suggests a wide variety of tasks:

  1 *Advisory positions:* Evaluator, fund raiser, needs assessor, proposal writer.
  2 *Administrative/clerical positions:* Typist, receptionist, clerk, supervisor.
  3 *Instructional positions:* Materials specialist, diagnostician, trainer, teacher aide, tutor.
  4 *Ancillary service positions:* Transportation worker, child care specialist, food worker, leisure-time worker.
  5 *Specialty positions:* Reading specialist, artist, journalist, researcher, public relations agent, counselor.

Listing Tasks

For the purpose of analyzing tasks, let us select five roles from the above list and specify the tasks involved: proposal writer, receptionist, tutor, transportation coordinator, and public relations agent. Many approaches are possible to analyze these roles. One way is to isolate many of the tasks that constitute a role. For this type of task analysis, Mager and Beach offer a schema (Figure 5-1) that proposes such factors as frequency of performance and importance to the job.[1] For determining volunteer posi-

---

[1]Robert F. Mager and Kenneth M. Beach, Jr., *Developing Vocational Instruction,* Fearon, Palo Alto, Calif., 1967, p. 13.

VOLUNTEER POSITION: _____

NO.	TASK	FREQUENCY OF PERFORMANCE	IMPORTANCE	REQUIRED EXPERTISE

Figure 5-1   Task listing sheet. *(Adapted from Robert F. Mager and Kenneth M. Beach, Jr., Developing Vocational Instruction, Fearon Publishers, Inc., Palo Alto, Calif., 1967, p. 13.)*

tions, Mager and Beach's third factor, learning difficulty, has been replaced by required expertise. These factors can be clarified through talking with paid staff in an organization. Mager and Beach further suggest that tasks be interpreted as sequential activities. Such a schema may have value, particularly for a new volunteer coordinator, when utilized as a method of analyzing roles for the purpose of building job descriptions.

Frequency of Performance   This category is used to determine how often a task is to be performed (daily, weekly, monthly). When frequency cannot be readily determined, an educated estimate can be made. Undoubtedly a potential volunteer would welcome knowledge concerning how often tasks are performed.

Importance   This signifies the differing levels of importance to be assigned to tasks. Some will always be more crucial than others. Mager and Beach suggest noting importance levels on a scale of 1 (high importance) to 3 (low importance), judged according to experience and available research.[2]

Required Expertise   This indicates the level of proficiency required to perform a task. If a certain task requires a high level of expertise, it may be desirable to recruit a person who possesses the necessary proficiency. Another option is to design a training program that will enable volunteers to overcome the difficulty. Judgment of the nature and extent of the ex-

[2]Ibid., p. 14.

pertise required for a given task can be aided by discussions with students or with experts in the area of difficulty.

Application of the formula outlined above makes it possible to specify tasks and their characterisitics as they relate to five examples of volunteer roles (Figure 5-2). It should be noted that judgments made as to frequency of performance, importance, and required expertise should be regarded as guidelines (and not precise conclusions) because these judgments will vary from person to person and program to program.

The job analyses found in Figure 5-2 are based on case studies of volunteer-based adult education programs served by the Illinois Region I Adult Education Service Center in the greater Chicago area. These volunteer jobs exist in a county jail, a senior citizens program, a community college, a museum, and a literacy project, respectively.

Detailing Tasks

The next step in Mager and Beach's analysis involves sequencing the parts, or steps, required in each task (Figure 5-3).[3] To do so calls for analyzing tasks according to optimum performance criteria. For example, the task of preparing a brochure may require several steps, such as writing copy, getting it approved, and working with the printer. These steps would be recorded in the second column of Figure 5-3.

Type of Performance   Mager and Beach present five kinds of performance, adapted from Robert Gagné's eight categories of learning:[4]

1 *Discrimination,* or knowing the difference between two or more things, conditions, or events (such as student skill level).
※ **2** *Problem solving,* or perceiving the solution to a problem (such as lesson design).
3 *Recall,* or knowing what to do based on experience or knowledge (such as knowing how to conduct a lesson).
4 *Manipulation,* or having the ability to perform a task (such as actually conducting a lesson).
5 *Communication,* knowing how to speak and write (such as communicating to a group).

What type of skills will a volunteer require to fulfill the assigned tasks? Distinguishing the type of performance is useful for selecting instructional strategies in preservice and in-service training.

Required Expertise   This is similar to the last column in Figure 5-2 in requiring judgments to be made about whether the steps are of high, mod-

[3]Ibid., pp. 18–24.
[4]Ibid., pp. 45–51. See also R. M. Gagné, *The Conditions of Learning,* rev. ed., Holt, Rinehart and Winston, New York, 1970, pp. 63–64.

VOLUNTEER POSITION: Proposal writer

NO.	TASK	FREQUENCY OF PERFORMANCE	IMPORTANCE	REQUIRED EXPERTISE
1.	Identify needs	Quarterly	1	High
2.	Seek advice and consent	Weekly	1	Low
3.	Identify sources	Quarterly	1	Moderate
4.	Secure guidelines	Quarterly	1	Low
5.	Write needs assessment	Monthly	1	High
6.	Write objectives	Monthly	1	High
7.	Associate objectives with activities	Monthly	1	High
8.	Prepare budget	Monthly	1	High
9.	Assemble and disseminate proposals	Monthly	1	Low
10.	Follow up on proposal decision	Monthly	1	Moderate
11.	Act upon final decision	Monthly	1	Moderate

VOLUNTEER POSITION: Receptionist

NO.	TASK	FREQUENCY OF PERFORMANCE	IMPORTANCE	REQUIRED EXPERTISE
1.	Answer phone	10–20 times daily	1	Low
2.	Greet visitors	6–10 times daily	1	Moderate
3.	Take and direct messages	10–20 times daily	1	Low
4.	Provide information	10–20 times daily	1	High
5.	Attend staff meetings	Weekly	3	Low
6.	Maintain office schedule	Weekly	2	Moderate
7.	Maintain records	Weekly	2	Moderate

VOLUNTEER POSITION: Tutor

NO.	TASK	FREQUENCY OF PERFORMANCE	IMPORTANCE	REQUIRED EXPERTISE
1.	Conduct initial interview and make diagnosis	Initial session	1	High
2.	Determine student goals and interests	Initial session	1	High
3.	Determine placement	Initial session	1	Moderate
4.	Select materials	As appropriate	1	High
5.	Choose methods and techniques	As appropriate	1	High
6.	Select appropriate setting	Initially	2	Low
7.	Determine schedule	Initially	1	Low
8.	Meet with students	Weekly	1	Low
9.	Evaluate student progress	Monthly	2	Moderate
10.	Prepare periodic reports	Monthly	3	Low
11.	Refer students	Upon termination of task	2	Moderate
12.	Attend training sessions	Monthly	2	Moderate

VOLUNTEER POSITION: Transportation coordinator

NO.	TASK	FREQUENCY OF PERFORMANCE	IMPORTANCE	REQUIRED EXPERTISE
1.	Maintain map of area served, chart routes	Weekly	2	Moderate
2.	Know clients' schedules	Weekly	1	Low
3.	Coordinate car-pooling	Weekly	1	Moderate
4.	Drive mini-van	Daily	1	Moderate
5.	Prepare reports	Monthly	2	Low
6.	Attend staff meetings	Weekly	3	Low

VOLUNTEER POSITION: Agency public relations agent

NO.	TASK	FREQUENCY OF PERFORMANCE	IMPORTANCE	REQUIRED EXPERTISE
1.	Assist in writing objectives	Annually	2	Moderate
2.	Prepare brochure	Annually	1	High
3.	Select audiences	Quarterly	2	Moderate
4.	Select methods and techniques	Monthly	2	Moderate
5.	Establish liaisons	Monthly	1	High
6.	Arrange speaking accommodation	Monthly	1	Moderate
7.	Assessing and making reports following events	Monthly	2	Moderate
8.	Evaluate success	Biannually	1	High
9.	Periodic meetings with administration	Weekly	2	Low
10.	Attend training sessions	Monthly	2	Moderate
11.	Submit periodic reports	Monthly	2	Low

Figure 5-2 *(Opposite and above)* Task-listing sheet.

JOB: _____

TASK: _____

NO.	STEPS IN PERFORMING TASK	TYPE OF PERFORMANCE	REQUIRED EXPERTISE

Figure 5-3 Task-detailing sheet.

JOB: Proposal writing

TASK: Prepare narrative of proposal

NO.	STEPS IN PERFORMING TASK	TYPE OF PERFORMANCE	REQUIRED EXPERTISE
1.	Understand funding guidelines and instructions	Problem solving	Moderate
2.	Refresh knowledge of philosophy and goals of the program	Recall	Moderate
3.	Meet with administrators	Problem solving	Low
4.	Recognize limitations of funding	Discrimination	Moderate
5.	Understand needs of population to be served	Problem solving	High
6.	Understand existing program coverage of need	Discrimination	Moderate
7.	Write the narrative	Communication	High

JOB: Receptionist

TASK: Take messages

NO.	STEPS IN PERFORMING TASK	TYPE OF PERFORMANCE	REQUIRED EXPERTISE
1.	Answer phone appropriately	Recall and discrimination	Low
2.	Ask caller to identify self	Communication	Low
3.	Determine nature and urgency of business	Communication	Low
4.	Determine whether caller will call back, requests a return call, or wants to leave information	Problem solving	Low
5.	Record message, instructions	Manipulation	Low
6.	Leave message in appropriate place	Manipulation	Low

JOB: Tutor

TASK: Initial interview and diagnosis

NO.	STEPS IN PERFORMING TASK	TYPE OF PERFORMANCE	REQUIRED EXPERTISE
1.	Solicit background information	Communication	Moderate
2.	Explain process, answer questions, address fears and apprehensions	Communication	Low
3.	Solicit students' goals	Communication	High
4.	Solicit students' interests	Communication	Moderate
5.	Record information	Communication	Low
6.	Prepare student for diagnosis	Communication	High
7.	Administer diagnosis	Recall	Moderate
8.	Interpret results	Discrimination	Moderate
9.	Share results with students	Communication	Moderate
10.	Establish goals of tutoring	Problem solving	High

JOB: Transportation coordinator

TASK: Maintain map of area served, chart results

NO.	STEPS IN PERFORMING TASK	TYPE OF PERFORMANCE	REQUIRED EXPERTISE
1.	Acquire large map of area served	Manipulation	Low
2.	Request clients' address from central office	Communication	Low
3.	Place tacks on map indicating where clients live	Manipulation	Low
4.	Determine most efficient routes	Problem solving	Moderate
5.	Update list and map as needed	Recall	Low
6.	Canvass information about available, reasonably priced types of transportation	Problem solving	Low

JOB: Agency public relations agent

TASK: Prepare brochure

NO.	STEPS IN PERFORMING TASK	TYPE OF PERFORMANCE	REQUIRED EXPERTISE
1.	Check accuracy of knowledge of program	Recall	Moderate
2.	Write copy for brochure	Communication	High
3.	Submit copy to others for criticism	Discrimination	Low
4.	Determine brochure length, size, type, the number to be printed, and schedule	Problem solving	Moderate
5.	Submit copy to printer for estimates	Problem solving	Moderate
6.	Submit budget estimates to volunteer coordinator for approval	Communication	Low
7.	Submit copy to printer for printing	Discrimination	Moderate
8.	Check proofs	Discrimination	High
9.	Disseminate brochures	Manipulation	Low

Figure 5-4 *(Opposite and above)* Task-detailing sheet.

erate, or low difficulty. It should be noted that the selected tasks appearing on the task listing sheets have been used in Figure 5-4.

One advantage of analyzing volunteer roles by breaking down tasks into smaller units of information, or steps, is that it helps potential volunteers make more informed choices on becoming a volunteer than would be the case if positions were merely announced. The information is also helpful to recruiters and may strongly influence their decisions concerning who is to be recruited. For example, if it is found that certain tasks (such as proposal writing) involve a high degree of difficulty, and if the program has neither the capacity nor the time in which to provide training, then it becomes necessary to recruit volunteers who already possess the expertise. For tasks which have a moderate level of difficulty (such as agency public relations agent), perhaps training could be provided, though volunteers who possess experience may be favored. In short, the difficulty posed by a certain task influences both the kind of volunteers to be recruited and the type of training needed. As for who is responsible for task analysis, it may be contingent on the type of climate. For example, in an open climate, the approach may be a collaborative one in which paid staff, volunteers, and a volunteer coordinator share in analyzing roles.

WRITING JOB DESCRIPTIONS

Job descriptions consist of carefully constructed statements that commonly reflect the mission and purpose of an organization, as they define the tasks assigned to volunteers. Some purposes of written job descriptions follow:

1   They define job responsibilities.
2   They supply supervisors and paid staff with job content information.
3   They allow volunteers to make an informed decision.
4   They facilitate the recruitment and placement of volunteers.
5   They suggest areas of training needed for effective job performance.
6   They lay a foundation for the supervision and evaluation of the volunteer job performance.

Ideally, job descriptions are written after program goals have been established and before recruitment begins. They are intended to be flexible, so that if certain goals and responsibilities receive new priorities, job descriptions can be changed. Often they include qualification requirements such as education, experience, an expertise which may automatically limit the number of potential applicants. To return to the example of proposal writer, a program may seek a college graduate who has had experience with social agencies and possesses writing ability. If few people apply, one option is to lessen the qualification requirements and provide on-the-job training. Another option is to limit the responsibilities of the position. However, either option places increased constraints on the organization.

Job descriptions often include summary statements about working conditions, including days and hours involved, duration of service, listing of available training opportunities, available leisure or expressive opportunities (such as use of facilities, activities, or subscription to services), and available ancillary services (such as child care, transportation, food service, or insurance). A statement of working conditions might also include a volunteer's degree of responsibility (including decision-making responsibility), opportunities to learn new skills, or degree of job flexibility in terms of time. All this information helps to specify the nature of the volunteer experience. Sample job descriptions appear in Appendix B.

POTENTIAL SOURCES OF VOLUNTEERS

A potential source of volunteers is highly dependent upon the type of program, the nature of the positions (including the expertise required), and the number of volunteers needed. Certain programs may prefer to be selective, particularly if special skills are required or if volunteers are to be recruited only from local colleges and universities. Some programs may deem it important to form a collaborative network with other social service agencies and share the recruitment process.

Who volunteers? The stereotype of a typical volunteer is a white, middle-class housewife between the ages of 28 and 42, with a college diploma, a car, and two children. However, helped by the changing status of women and of volunteering itself, this activity is attracting people of all ages from all parts of the community and from all races. No age group, sex, race, or socioeconomic group should be ruled out as sources of volunteers. It is wise to avoid building mental barriers that exclude certain segments of the population because volunteering is simply not an activity reserved for special groups.

The following list of institutions, organizations, and agencies may be helpful as sources for recruiting volunteers. The great diversity of purposes and activities represented here affords some hint of the variety of people who elect to become volunteers.

Voluntary Action Centers	Antipoverty programs
Local high schools	Neighborhood Youth Corps
Local business and industry	Public affairs offices
Universities and colleges	YMCA and YWCA
Voluntary bureaus	Welfare councils
Religious organizations	Alumni associations
Retired citizen organizations	Head Start programs
Parent-teacher associations	Block clubs
Civic organizations	Employment services
Professional and community	Friends of paid staff
organizations	VISTA
Service clubs	CETA
Fraternal clubs	Political groups
Tenant councils	

To single out one popular source of volunteers, university and high school students are often dedicated and capable volunteers whose enthusiasm can add much to the morale of an agency. In return, an agency can sometimes offer students inducements in the form of credit or pertinent experience, although student availability will vary with examinations and vacations. It is important to arrange realistic commitments with students, perhaps through a campus internship adviser.

Another group, business and industry, has become increasingly involved in community affairs. Hence, personnel directors are often good sources for contacting volunteers, especially if they maintain lists of employees willing to volunteer, act as brokers for placement, and/or issue in-house newsletters that give notice of voluntary opportunities for employees. As automation pervades the production and manufacturing industries, and as employment patterns shift, increased amounts of leisure time might compel workers to seek volunteer work as an activity which offers genuine fulfillment.

METHODS OF RECRUITMENT

As a general rule, specific methods are preferred to the haphazard recruitment of volunteers. Whenever possible, it is wise to choose recruitment methods that are based on a knowledge of the group to be selected. Often, successful recruiting techniques require person-to-person contact. In order to deal with specific questions from potential volunteers, it is important for a recruiter to have a firm understanding of a program—its goals, strengths, and weaknesses. He or she should also be prepared to deal honestly with the advantages and disadvantages of being associated with it. The logistics, such as the amount of time involved, availability of transportation, and proximity of places to eat, are also important.

What characterisitics distinguish an excellent recruiter from an adequate one? The following list suggests some answers; an excellent recruiter:

1 Identifies with the target group, that is, has knowledge of the folkways, mores, and history of the group or groups being recruited.
2 Knows the objectives, procedures, and parameters of a program.
3 Understands the community, institutions, and resources.
4 Can communicate, on the basis of empathy, with a wide range of people.
5 Is committed to the goals of a volunteer-based program.
6 Believes in lifelong learning for self and for others.

When a recruiter is not available, who should recruit? Given the characteristics stated above, it is obvious that not everyone can qualify as a recruiter. Some people regard recruitment as an unpleasant task and, in that case, the responsibility should be reserved for those who enjoy meeting new people and helping the program grow.

Sometimes collaborative networks are formed among several agencies for the purpose of collective recruitment drives. Such networks not only offer cost savings but also provide benefits such as sharing of ideas and pooling of talents. In this arrangement, good timing is essential, especially if the agencies operate on varying fiscal years. For example, a university may act as a broker, assuming responsibility for schedule, objectives, and duration of a recruitment campaign. If students are to be recruited, the agencies will have to conform jointly to the school calendar. Other possible brokers include the Voluntary Action Center, social and religious organizations, and public schools.

The selection of promotional methods requires a recruiter to concentrate on the type of person sought, the nature of a program, and the availability of funding. Some techniques are designed to create general interest and awareness, whereas others make a direct appeal for a specific commitment. We will next discuss two techniques: mass recruitment and personalized recruitment. For specialized positions, such as proposal writer, recruiter, or typist, personalized recruitment is suggested.

Mass Recruitment

The following methods are useful for creating awareness of and interest in a new program.

Newspaper   Some techniques are free, such as press releases, feature stories, and letters to the editor; others are budget items, such as classified and picture advertisements. Press releases centering around human interest stories, unique activities, and interesting people may find a willing response from newspapers and attract public interest. Convincing feature stories are useful for creating general awareness, especially if pictures are included. Possible topics include historical trends, personality profiles, or community concerns. Advertisements are more likely to receive prime space as well as a more accurate depiction.

Small News Sources   Trade and association newsletters are effective for reaching specific audiences. Press releases issued to newletters are most effective when the issues addressed are of particular interest to readers.

Brochures, Flyers, and Posters   Used in post offices, libraries, doctor's offices, supermarkets, and other public places, these materials create general awareness of a program.

Public Service Announcements on Radio or TV   If honest and believable, such announcements can be successful. If the station's schedule permits, a manager may air the announcement as a public service. However, competition for public-service air time is fierce.

Interviews on Radio or TV   Appearances by articulate persons on radio or television can be effective in reaching particular audiences. In planning interviews, it is important to consider who watches or listens to a station during the time of the broadcasts.

Mailers   Mailers are often used to announce a new program, its nature and scope, and the advantages of volunteering for it. However, the production and mailing costs of a well-designed flyer may be prohibitive.

Speaking Engagements   Group contact has the advantage of enabling interested persons to ask specific questions. It also allows a recruiter to address any concerns expressed by those in the audience.

Open Houses and Tours   On-site group contact offers recruiters the chance to show the actual resources and facilities that a program has to offer. Such activities should be followed up by letters and phone calls. Further awareness can be stimulated by involving the press.

Personalized Recruitment

Door-to-Door   Door-to-door recruitment has the advantage of being highly personal, making it possible to address specific concerns. The recruiter using this method must be able to gain the trust of people. Follow-up activities are important.

Personal Letters and Phone Calls   Following a meeting, open house, or visit, a letter or a phone call serves as a useful reminder.

Bring-a-Friend Night   This method seems most effective when volunteers themselves bring the friends and do the talking.

CONCLUSION

The emphasis in this chapter has been on preplanning in the recruitment process. The approach begins with determination of the roles and responsibilities of volunteers and specification of the tasks involved. Next, material such as job descriptions must be carefully prepared, outlining the conditions of the job to potential volunteers. Only after these details have been worked out and recruitment methods and techniques chosen should contact with the public be made. On the assumption that there are capable people ready and willing to volunteer, it becomes the responsibility of program recruiters to initiate contacts with prospective volunteers and give them the information they need to make wise decisions. Ultimately, perhaps, the degree of success realized by recruiters depends upon the reputation that a program has gained within a community.

Selection, Orientation, Placement, and Training of Volunteers

INTRODUCTION

In the preceding chapter, the point was made that the more precision and special skill required in a job, the more care must be given to directing recruitment efforts toward selected populations. The next steps to be taken to increase the likelihood of proper placement are selection, orientation, and training. For example, if volunteers are to be placed with senior citizens for the purpose of facilitating leisure activities, it is important to avoid placing volunteers who have misconceptions about the physiological or psychological characteristics of the aging. Such misconceptions may lead volunteers to adopt patronizing attitudes toward the elderly. Such situations should be avoided through careful selection. Interviews would help to reveal whether candidates entertain misconceptions, and potential volunteers could be accepted or rejected accordingly. Another way to deal with the problem is through training. All applicants would be accepted and, prior to placement, would attend a seminar aimed at possibly overcoming minor misconceptions. Volunteers who successfully completed the seminar would then be placed. It is recognized, of course, that ensuring suitable volunteers involves more than single-factor selection.

The above example demonstrates the similar intentions that lie behind the activities of selection and training—to facilitate the highest possible degree of productivity of volunteers in a program. The purpose of this chapter is to outline the methods volunteer coordinators can use to maximize the performance levels of volunteers. Correct placement and high productivity not only involve awareness of the managerial activities associated with selection, orientation, and training but also depend upon matching the goals, interests, and abilities of volunteers to the tasks to be performed. Specifically, this chapter will explore the application, interview, selection decision, agreement concerning employment conditions, orientation, preservice training, placement, and in-service training.

THE APPLICATION

Application forms constitute a means of seeking and storing pertinent information regarding the qualifications, goals, and experience of volunteer candidates. This information serves a useful purpose not only in the selection process but also in the training, placement, and supervision processes. For many volunteer-based programs, the application is the first step in the selection process.

In designing application forms, it is important to obtain all the basic data about candidates (name, address, education, experience). Attempts should be made to determine special interests and aptitudes, other commitments, time schedules, and a candidate's motives for volunteering.

In Figure 6-1 the categories of information are not meant to be ex-

Categories	Item
Background information	• Name, address, phone number
	• Days, hours available
	• Mode of transportation
Education and experience	• Employment experience
	• Volunteer experience
	• References
	• Educational level
	• Fluency in foreign language (if relevant)
	• Travel experience
Interests, goals and expectations	• Interests and hobbies
	• Reasons for volunteering
	• Area of volunteer interest
	• Knowledge of and skills in service area
	• Short- and long-range career goals
	• Educational goals (if relevant)
	• Expectations from organization

Figure 6-1 Application information.

1. Name: _____   3. Phone: _____
2. Address: _____   Work: _____
   _____   Home: _____
   _____

4. What are your reasons for volunteering? (Use the back if necessary.) _____
   _____
   _____
   _____

5. What expectations do you have of the organization? _____
   _____
   _____

6. What academic degrees have you earned? _____
   _____

7. What academic experiences will help you as a volunteer? _____
   _____
   _____

8. What is (are) your current job(s), including volunteer work? _____
   _____
   _____

9. What employment experience will help you as a volunteer? _____
   _____
   _____

10. What are your interests and hobbies? _____
   _____

11. How many hours per week can you commit as a volunteer? (Please list in the chart below.)
    Days: _____   Times: _____
          _____   _____
          _____   _____
          _____   _____   Total hours: _____
12. Do you have a valid driver's license? _____
13. When can you begin volunteering? _____

Figure 6-2   Volunteer application.

haustive, but should provide a guide for constructing a purposeful application form that will elicit needed information about prospective volunteers. When collecting information about an applicant, job descriptions and requirements should be kept in mind. For specific jobs, it may be advisable to construct special forms. A sample volunteer application can be found in Figure 6-2.

THE INTERVIEW

Interviews are two-way information exchanges that normally follow the completion of application forms. Interviews are useful to recruiters in expanding information contained in the forms and in gaining information that the forms might have neglected, such as the attitudes, beliefs, and motives of prospective volunteers. Interviews also provide applicants with opportunities to learn about an organization and to make judgments concerning their involvement in it. They become future-oriented through discussions of policies, procedures, and norms of the organization. Finally, interviews provide input to program planners for the expansion of existing jobs or the creation of new ones, especially when it is discovered that some volunteers possess skills and ambitions beyond those envisaged in job descriptions. Or the discovery of discrepancies in volunteer skills or attitudes could affect the determination of training objectives.

The skill of the interviewer is perhaps the most important factor for a successful interview. An unknowledgeable and unpracticed person in that position could possibly negate even the most carefully planned strategy. A firm understanding of the practices and policies of an organization, as well as a reasoned predetermination of the direction of the interview, increases the likelihood of a successful interview.

Obviously, a major purpose in interviewing is to forecast, as accurately as possible, the performance of applicants. What kind of information should we seek to determine a volunteer candidate's potential? Although predicting a person's behavior is a risky proposition, it seems reasonable to judge a candidate's future performance on the basis of past attitudes and behavior, including working habits. For example, if it found that an applicant has long demonstrated a desire to learn, or that he or she consistently works well with others, these might be construed as powerful indicators of success as a volunteer. The nature and length of prior commitments, especially in volunteer work, records of civic or community involvement, and reasons for leaving previous employment may provide insights about future performance. Any judgments should take situational variables into account. For example, a person may have had to leave school in order to help support a family, or a person may have lived in numerous localities because of job transfers.

How can interviews be structured so as to uncover this information in a tactful way? Some suggested guidelines and pitfalls are presented in Figure 6-3.

As suggested in the preceding section, it is helpful to have thought through the kind of skills, attitudes, or knowledge desired by candidates when seeking information for selection purposes. Once these have been determined, the next step is to decide how information will be sought. Figure 6-4 provides a sample listing of questions grouped under possible areas of inquiry.[1] Many questions will not only elicit facts but will also yield insights into personality characteristics (for example, the

[1] Adapted from Marlene Wilson, *Effective Management of Volunteer Programs,* Volunteer Management Associates, Boulder, Colo. 1977, pp. 130–133.

Guidelines	Pitfalls
Setting the stage for the interview	
1. Choose a relaxed, comfortable environment which encourages a spirit of honesty and openness.	1. Avoid a busy environment where frequent interruptions cause an interviewee to feel nervous or distracted.
2. Listen attentively while being mindful of the flow of conversation, emerging patterns of experience, nonverbal or body language.	2. Refrain from putting the interviewee on the defensive with insistent interrogation or patronizing questions.
Strategies for questioning	
1. Ask open-ended questions which encourage narrative responses and thoughtful analysis. Try to ask questions in such a way that an interviewee feels that several options are available.	1. Avoid questions that demand only "Yes" or "No" answers or questions that put words into the interviewee's mouth.
2. Use probing questions to obtain clarification of issues.	2. Abstain from rude or brusque behavior in seeking further information.
The interview process	
1. Be prepared to explain the details of a particular assignment and the purposes of a program.	1. Avoid rushing through the interview.
2. Try to build rapport by showing understanding and consideration toward the interviewee.	2. Refrain from assuming a rigid, threatening, or overbearing stance.
3. Know what kind of information you are looking for, but be alert to securing additional information which might be of service to a program.	3. Avoid having either no plan or an inflexible one.

Figure 6-3 Interviewing strategies.

interviewee's sense of self-worth) and attitudes toward authority, learning, and assuming responsibility.

THE SELECTION DECISION

Whether information about volunteers is gained through an application form, an interview, or both, it is wise to process that information systematically so that biases do not creep in. While first impressions may be important, they should be checked against the information that is accumulated. The following selection pitfalls are to be avoided:

Patterns of employment experience
1. What responsibilities have you had in former paid jobs or volunteer jobs?
2. What other experiences do you bring to the position?
3. How would you describe your work habits?
4. What is the ideal job for you?
5. What were some of your likes and dislikes in former positions?
6. Why did you leave your last job?
7. How do you think you can help us?
8. What experience have you had in working with adults?

Motives for volunteering
1. Why did you choose this organization?
2. To what extent can you commit yourself at this time?
3. Why do you want to volunteer?
4. What are some of your short- and long-range personal goals? What are your educational goals?
5. What do you know about this organization?
6. Is there anything in particular that you want to learn while on this job?
7. What do you enjoy most about volunteering?
8. What do you enjoy least about volunteering?
9. What kinds of people do you most enjoy working with?
10. What kinds of people do you have difficulty working with?
11. What is it that attracts you to this particular area of adult education?
12. What do you hope to gain from it?

Figure 6-4 Interview guide.

1   The candidate is accepted or rejected because he or she shares interests or background—such as travel experience, place of residence, or alma mater—with the interviewer. Rather, the candidate should be accepted or rejected on such factors as skill, attitude, knowledge, and potential.

2   Making decisions hastily should be avoided. Instead, decisions should be made carefully.

3   The decision is made soon after the interview begins, on the grounds that the candidate is very personable. Personality may be only one factor. Other evidence should be culled before a decision is reached.

4   The interviewer's values influence the decision to an unwarranted extent. Preferably, an interviewer will remain open to a variety of life styles, thereby keeping an open mind.

5   The candidate's mannerisms unduly affect the selection decision.

On the contrary, judgments concerning a candidate's potential should be made on reasoned criteria without interference from biases.

Inviting staff members or volunteers to join in the selection process can be helpful. It also allows them to become involved in the decision-making aspects of a program.

AGREEMENT ON EMPLOYMENT CONDITIONS

Once a volunteer has been accepted, an agreement serves to formalize expectations. There is no question that a mutually beneficial experience depends upon a volunteer's success in fulfilling the expectations placed on him or her by an organization and its success in meeting a volunteer's expectations. The agreement, preferably a written document, will contain factors of importance to a volunteer, such as working conditions, fringe benefits, and training options. It will also outline standards of performance which an organization considers vital, such as hours of work per week, duration of service, performance indicators, and required training or attendance at meetings. In effect, an agreement is an expansion of the job description. In general, an organization expects reliable performance from volunteers, the provision of a certain amount of time, and the discharging of duties in a prescribed way. A volunteer expects to be treated fairly, to be given opportunities to perform worthwhile work, to learn new skills, and to occupy a definable area of responsibility. The value of an agreement as a bond between an organization and a volunteer is that it may shape the behavior of volunteers and of those working with them. It can also serve as an evaluative and supervising device.

Different types of volunteer organizations require different types of agreements, depending upon the degree of formality, the ends and means of an organization, and the tasks to be performed. It would seem more appropriate, for example, for an agreement to be written for volunteer nurses than it would for volunteers in a religious setting, because the responsibilities and procedures are more clearly defined in the former situation. In less precise situations, like a community bake sale, a verbal agreement might suffice. It is the intent behind the agreement which serves the purpose, and not necessarily the means by which it is done.

What if a volunteer is uncertain about his or her expectations? Such a situation is commonplace, the implication being that an agreement cannot be concluded hastily. Instead, an effort should be made to carefully review a volunteer's experience and background in relation to an organization's goals and expectations.

As mentioned earlier, an agreement consists of two parts: a volunteer's expectations of an organization and its expectations of a volunteer. What volunteers can expect (see Figure 6-5) can be categorized as organizational cooperation, ancillary benefits, humanistic considerations, and opportunities for learning. What an organization can expect (see Figure 6-6) can be categorized as organizational requirements, time commitment, attitudinal considerations, and standards of success.

In Figure 6-5 organizational cooperation refers to an organization's willingness to share its resources confidently with volunteers and to plan

Organizational cooperation
1. Access to facilities
2. Access to organizational leaders
3. Safe working conditions
4. Interaction with others
5. Opportunities for advancement
6. Opportunities for leadership or decision making
7. Access to information about an organization
8. Chance to be involved in worthwhile tasks
9. Chance to be challenged with meaningful assignments
10. Chance to learn the job when the time is right
11. Awareness of organizational constraints

Ancillary benefits
1. Reimbursement for travel
2. Reimbursement for courses or workshops
3. Child care support
4. Insurance options
5. Participation in organizational activities, such as sports or cultural events
6. Visitation rights in a hospital or jail

Humanistic considerations
1. To be treated with respect, as a dedicated employee
2. To be offered an open social climate
3. To be recognized for efficient performance
4. To be evaluated and supervised fairly
5. To be assured that a volunteer's opinion is important

Opportunities for learning
1. Being placed in a learning environment
2. Preservice training
3. In-service training
4. Access to courses of formal instruction
5. Access to instructional materials
6. Special seminars or conferences

Figure 6-5 Elements of the agreement of employment conditions: What a volunteer can expect.

experiences that will promote their personal and professional growth. Ancillary benefits can assume importance for volunteers by easing their worries about transportation, child care, or the cost of taking courses and by assuring them of their status in an organization. Many items are specific to certain organizations, such as uniforms for Red Cross volunteers, special exhibit tickets for museum volunteers, or tuition waivers for community college volunteers.

Humanistic considerations denote the respect given volunteers as employees and individuals, and the guidance and moral support which accompanies such respect. Included in this category are ethical considerations relating to status, responsibility, and recognition.

Opportunities for learning embrace the chance to gain new skills, knowledge, or attitudes through workshops or other means. Learning often acts as a powerful incentive for volunteer participation and may even induce volunteers to commit themselves to an organization.

In Figure 6-6, organizational requirements are those which help to acquaint volunteers with the internal structure and functioning of an organization and the volunteer's place in it. Time commitment refers to the frequency and duration of service which a volunteer is prepared to make to an organization. Attitudinal considerations denote an organization's perception of desirable qualities of volunteers, especially their devotion to its goals. Standards of success relate to performance of volunteers and may be relatively easy to define in a hospital or correctional institutional setting, where the limits of volunteer service can be clearly defined.

Not all categories need be included in all agreements. The decision depends upon such factors as the personal styles of a volunteer and a volunteer coordinator and what an organization can tolerate (i.e., the type of special privileges allowed a volunteer, the nature of a volunteer posi-

---

Organizational requirements
1. Efficient record keeping
2. Attendance at mandatory meetings or training sessions
3. Knowledge of organization function
4. Understanding of hierarchy, particularly supervisory positions
5. Understanding of responsibilities, obligations, privileges, and power
6. Understanding of patterns of coordination
7. Understanding of goals of volunteer-based program
8. Understanding of lines of authority

Time commitment
1. Number of hours to be served per week
2. Length of service
3. Special expectations, as dictated by tasks assigned to volunteers

Attitudinal considerations
1. To be committed to the goals and standards of an organization
2. To work in a spirit of diligence and service
3. To be dedicated to assigned tasks
4. To exercise loyalty and discretion in communicating information about an organization to others

Standards of success
1. Goals of assignment
2. Evaluation criteria
3. Special competencies required
4. Limitations of area to be served
5. Knowledge requirements

Figure 6-6 Elements of the agreement of employment conditions: What an organization can expect.

tion, or the availability of funds for fringe benefits). An ideal agreement is, of course, one which responds to the specific needs of both an organization and a volunteer.

ORIENTATION

During orientation, volunteers become aware of the policies, procedures, and philosophy of the organization; its expectations concerning their roles; and the history and traditions of a volunteer-based program. In addition, volunteers become acquainted with paid staff and their functions in an organization. Through this process, with its salutary effect of dispelling volunteers' confusion and anxiety, it is expected that a firm commitment to the goals of an organization will develop. On the other hand, the process will prove valuable if it uncovers discrepancies between the desires of a volunteer and the demands of an organization; the best solution would then be for a volunteer to withdraw from pursuing activities with the organization.

Good communication is a primary ingredient in orientation. An astute volunteer coordinator will listen carefully to a volunteer's concerns and try to assess how these could be satisfied within the context of an organization's goals, available resources, needs of other volunteers and paid staff, and so on. Where a climate of trust prevails, relaxed and honest communication is likely to flourish, causing the learning needs of a volunteer to surface. The next step would be to base a training program on those needs. In effect, a volunteer might begin his or her training before placement.

Lastly, orientation provides broad clues for the proper placement of volunteers. If placement means matching their talents with program challenges, to the satisfaction of all concerned, then orientation plays a key role in that process.

Types of Orientation Programs

There may be commonalities in all orientation processes, but there is no "correct" way. The nature of a program, lines of authority, type of organization, the skill levels of volunteers—all contribute to differences in orientation programs. Some are individualized, others are conducted in large or small groups. Some are best organized by paid staff, others by a volunteer coordinator.

As for designing the content of orientation sessions, see the topics listed in Figure 6-7. Some will have been dealt with during the interview.

There are many ways to orient volunteers. It is important to choose the correct method based on personal style, skill level, and background of volunteers and the type of organization. Orienting volunteers can be done in the following ways:

Organizational functions
Population served
Types of programs
Location of activities
Resources and facilities

Organizational history
Founding date and circumstances (including mission statement or purpose)
Governing body
Expansion rate
Funding process
Change of focus or purpose
Numbers of people served
Early workers

Rules and regulations
Statutes or bylaws of organization
Existing codes of conduct for paid personnel, clients, volunteers
Reporting requirements
Health and safety requirements

Lines of authority
Hierarchy of organization
Communication channels
Nature of volunteer-based program
Status of volunteer-based program

Benefits and incentives
Policies regarding reimbursement for mileage, child care, and tuition
Special privileges given to volunteers
Social and recognition functions
Training programs

Volunteers' reactions
Concerns and fears of volunteers
Additional points raised by volunteers
General discussion with paid staff

Figure 6-7 Selected issues and topics of organization.

1 Large groups Orienting en masse saves time and is best employed when the information to be provided is simple. It is wise to involve paid staff, high-level decision makers, and other volunteers, whenever possible. In addition to being supportive, they can expand information or clarify points. The interaction between them and volunteers can promote understanding and reduce the possibility of conflict.

2 Small groups In small groups, people tend to voice their opinions more freely and come to know each other better, a situation that often creates a team spirit.

3 One-to-one relationships A one-to-one relationship between a volunteer coordinator and a volunteer creates an intimacy that makes

possible the planning of highly individualized training and placement programs. However, time and financial constraints sometimes work against this approach.

4 Independent study A volunteer could work independently if given specially designed materials, reading assignments, slides, and tapes (a do-it-yourself orientation kit), as well as a chance to observe. Clearly, the onus is on the volunteers. Provision must be made to answer the questions that will undoubtedly arise.

PLACEMENT

Placing a volunteer into a particular role occurs once his or her interests, skills, and inclinations have been discovered. It has been strongly implied that without thoughtful assessment of volunteers' skills, without provision for them to gain an understanding of an organization, placement becomes a matter of luck. Selection and orientation are, then, crucial to the placement of volunteers in positions where they can contribute to an organization while furthering their personal growth.

Where a job description and criteria for job selection are well-focused and orientation equips volunteers with attitudes and information necessary to understand the job, placement becomes relatively easy. When these conditions are not met, a probationary period may help in several ways: (1) volunteers can attest to their confidence in their ability to do the work; (2) program personnel can determine when volunteers are capable and, when not, can change assignments; and (3) the validity and reliability of the indicators of success can be assessed. In this sense, a probationary period can be mutually beneficial. Volunteers gain an opportunity to learn about various aspects of a program and the specific nature of their contributions and rewards, and program benefits from the involvement and feedback of personnel. When volunteer supervisors actually direct the placement process, there appears to be a greater chance for quicker and more lasting placement.

When volunteers cannot be placed immediately into the jobs of their choice, programs have been known to create new positions, develop waiting lists, or make referrals. Inviting volunteers to attend orientation or preservice training sessions has the advantage of building mutual familiarity for the future.

PRESERVICE AND IN-SERVICE TRAINING

Preservice training follows orientation and commonly precedes placement. Such training is intended to assess the abilities of volunteers and to equip them with the formal skills needed to perform their assignments. In short, preservice training consists of both assessment and training functions, and has obvious implications for placement.

The more sophisticated the assignment, the more necessary preservice training becomes. Once skills have been obtained, volunteers can move confidently into their areas of responsibility. To neglect such training would be to leave them unprepared and set the stage for the demise of a program.

Many of the guidelines envisaged for preservice training coincide with those for in-service training. However, preservice training is unique in that a volunteer's satisfaction, abilities, and performance can be assessed and acted upon prior to placement.

In-service training is a means to ensure volunteers' continued growth and to maintain job efficiency. Well-designed training is most effective after volunteers have been on a job for a period of time. According to Eva Shindler-Rainman and Ronald Lippitt, in-service aims at "maintenance of effort training" —removing volunteers from ruts, exchanging practices, and gaining new methods.[2] In addition, in-service training increases the potential of both volunteers and an organization. To be effective, in-service training must reflect volunteers' social and learning needs.

The following purposes for in-service training are suggested:

1   To reinforce skills, knowledge, and/or attitudes.
2   To introduce new skills, knowledge, and/or attitudes.
3   To plan and manage program changes.
4   To provide volunteers with opportunities for self-renewal and growth.
5   To provide assurance to paid staff and others that volunteers are receiving professional training.
6   To increase group rapport and teamwork.
7   To offer volunteers a forum in which to express their concerns.
8   To help volunteers and an organization reach their maximum potential.
9   To ensure, in as many ways as possible, that the purposes of an organization are aligned with the needs of volunteers.

Bringing the principles and processes of adult education to bear on the design of in-service training of volunteers involves a sequence of steps: needs assessment and program objectives, design and delivery of program content, the instructional process, implementation, and evaluation.

[2]Eva Schindler-Rainman and Ronald Lippitt, *The Volunteer Community: Creative Use of Human Resources*, NTL Learning Resource Corporation, Fairfax, Va., 1975, p. 72.

Needs Assessment and Program Objectives

As Malcolm Knowles demonstrates (see Figure 6-8), needs assessment means determining the needs of three groups: individuals (in this case, volunteers), the organization, and the community. Needs are closely related to interests, capabilities, and attitudes. To illustrate, in a crisis counseling center that employs volunteers, close interaction exists between the center and people in the community. It is apparent that volunteers need in-service training to equip them with skills in interpersonal relations. According to Knowles' schema, all such needs must pass through figurative "filters": institutional purposes (counseling of people in crises), feasibility, and interests of clientele (volunteers).

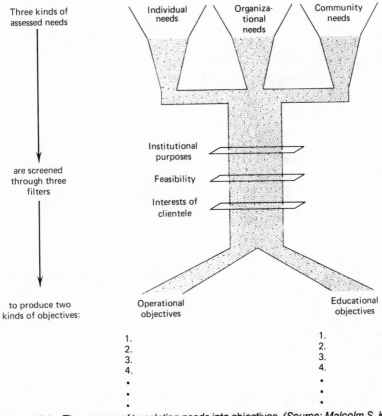

Figure 6-8   The process of translating needs into objectives. *(Source: Malcolm S. Knowles, The Modern Practice of Adult Education: Andragogy versus Pedagogy, Association Press, New York, 1970, p. 127. Used by permission of Association Press/Follett Publishing Company.)*

Purposes Needs which do not "fit" the purposes of a program should be screened out. In the case of the crisis center, volunteers' needs for training in interpersonal and communication skills would survive the first filter.

Feasibility The feasibility process often screens out the expenditure of large amounts of time and money. Examples are needs which call for elaborate training (such as learning psychological diagnostic procedures), costly equipment, an inordinate amount of space, or extensive travel. To return to the crisis center volunteers, their need to acquire skills in interpersonal relations would survive the feasibility filter if such training could take place under the tutelage of an instructor who could be hired for a reasonable fee.

Interests of Clientele Humanistic educators generally agree that learning quality is greatly influenced by a learner's level of interest. Adults are voluntary learners. Normally, they learn what they prefer to learn. It therefore behooves a planner of volunteer preservice and in-service training to consider the interests of the volunteers. At the same time, if an organization is to achieve its goals, the volunteer coordinator must ensure that volunteers possess the competencies needed for effective performance. Knowles suggests that one objective for training might be to heighten the interest levels of volunteers. To continue with the example of the crisis center, the need to instill interpersonal relations skills in volunteers would survive the interests-of-clientele filter if the content were of interest to volunteers.

Translating Needs into Objectives

According to Knowles, the needs that survive the filtering process can then be translated into operational and educational objectives. To facilitate implementation and evaluation, objectives should be measurable, clearly stated, and in written form. Operational objectives are those which "identify the things that will be done to improve the quality of instructional resources for meeting the educational needs."[3] Those resources include format, facilities, and logistics. Examples of operational objectives are:

1 To conduct three half-day sessions in the course of a year for the entire staff on the topic of interpersonal communications skills.
2 To reduce the dropout level.

[3]Malcolm S. Knowles, *The Modern Practice of Adult Education: Andragogy versus Pedagogy,* Association Press, New York, 1973, p. 126.

3 To organize a representative committee of between six and eleven people, composed of volunteers, paid staff, and administrators, for the purpose of planning and implementing in-service sessions and establishing evaluation procedures.

4 To provide transportation and child care services for volunteers during the sessions.

5 To reserve a reasonably priced site for the sessions that is away from telephones and other disturbances.

Educational objectives refer to learning opportunities extended to volunteers. Their value may be demonstrated later by increased performance, new skills, or higher level of understanding. Objectives which relate to the crisis center example and volunteers' needs for skill in interpersonal relations might read as follows. After attending three half-day sessions, volunteers will:

1 Show an ability to listen without interrupting.
2 Display nonthreatening interviewing skills.
3 Contribute confidently to group discussions.

Design and Delivery of Program Content

Once objectives have been formulated, attention can be given to the design and delivery of content under the headings of format or methods, site and facilities, and instructional process including human and other resources. The implied decisions to be made require early attention, based on volunteers' needs and interests, available funding, time, and the nature of the content.

Format or Methods Format, or methods, refers to the manner in which an organization plans to deliver a volunteer-based program. There are three approaches: individual, group, and community.

1 Individual
  a Apprenticeship
  b Internship
  c Correspondence study
  d Programmed instruction
  e Directed individual study
2 Group
  a Clinic, institute, or workshop
  b Class
  c Discussion group
  d Conference, convention, fair
3 Community
  a Community education

In these approaches, the relationship between learner and organization differs significantly. An important characteristic of the individual approach is a one-to-one relationship in the learning process. In the apprenticeship, this relationship takes place in a job setting where the learner acquires knowledge and has an opportunity to apply it. This approach to learning occurs under close instructional supervision. The internship, in contrast to the apprenticeship, takes place after the completion of formal study. In this one-to-one relationship, the learner has an opportunity to integrate knowledge and skills in a particular work role under the supervision of an expert. In correspondence study, the learner is isolated from the organization by such factors as geography and time. The format provides for systematic study at a distance through the use of correspondence and tapes. In contrast to this approach, programmed instruction links the learner to predesigned material in the form of a book, teaching machine, or computer. Finally, under directed individual study, the one-to-one relationship between the learner and the organization suggests some direct personal contact. Its use may take the form of suggesting materials for individual study. In some cases, it takes the form of adult counseling that furthers the learner's goals.

The group approaches suggest the simultaneous involvement of many learners in a learning activity. The clinic, institute, or workshop are methods used for a learning experience of short duration, usually 1 to 5 days. In many cases, the learners collaborate with staff in the design, direction, and application of the content presented. Unlike the clinic, institute, or workshop, the class is usually planned for a longer period of time. Although the organization and responsibility for the class content rests with the educator, this class format presents two extremes: teacher-centered and learner-centered. For some adult learning, the former may be preferred; for many others, the latter may be the most desirable. The conference, convention, or fair involves large-group methods which bring together many learners for a limited period of time. To meet the learning needs of this diverse audience, varied learning experiences are designed around a theme, slogan, or some other broad topic.

The community approach suggests a process whereby the community serves as the setting for its members to solve problems related to living. Here, it is important that the members of the community study their problems, a process which might lead them to take action. Recently, audio and videotape recorders have been used as interactive media to assist community members to determine probable priorities.

Site and Facilities The location of in-service training is commonly selected based on the convenience and availability of funds. Experienced planners of workshops and conferences recognize the importance of selecting a site that will enhance rather than inhibit the learning process. To this end, it is desirable that the following facilities be readily available:

1 Food service
2 Meeting rooms
3 Display area (if needed)
4 Adequate heat, ventilation, lighting, and acoustics
5 Absence of noise
6 Appropriate furniture for adults
7 Audiovisual equipment
8 Library facilities
9 Storage facilities
10 Parking and public transportation facilities

The Instructional Process and Implementation

The instructional process described below has the effect of implementing in-service training.

1 Develop a climate that will encourage volunteers to participate actively in the learning process.
2 Diagnose their learning problems, with special attention to physiological, psychological, and sociological differences that may affect motivation.
3 Help volunteers set attainable, measurable objectives, expressed in behavioral terms and based on their needs.
4 Develop materials and utilize a variety of techniques and devices (shown in detail in Appendix C and D) appropriate to subject matter.
5 Plan activities that bring community and other resources to bear on volunteers' needs.
6 Evaluate volunteers' performance and program effectiveness on objectives based on preassessment of volunteers.[4]

Evaluation

Evaluation entails qualitatively measuring the impact of in-service training on volunteers and program activities in order to improve subsequent training. It is an important step and one that will be treated extensively in Chapter 8.

CONCLUSION

It is hoped that this chapter will convey some sense of the time and energy associated with the activities of selection, orientation, placement, and training. The central theme is the suitability of volunteers for their ap-

[4]John A. Niemi and Catherine Davison, "The Adult Basic Education Teacher: A Model for the Analysis of Training," *Adult Leadership,* February 1971, p. 247.

pointed tasks and the ways in which an organization can inspire them to optimum performance. The selection process, with its communication flow between volunteer and organization, provides a valuable exchange of information which helps both sides to decide whether they could work fruitfully together for their mutual benefit. Orientation continues this flow and, at its best, produces a commitment by volunteers to the goals of the organization.

Placement matches volunteers to tasks appropriate to their capacities, while training provides for enhancing those capacities or adding new ones. This is not to say that all learning must be formal. Informal means such as observation and discussions with other volunteers may be equally helpful where certain topics are concerned. It must always be kept in mind that the processes of selection, orientation, placement, and training are interlocking units with a single purpose: to satisfy the needs of volunteers while simultaneously advancing the goals of an organization.

Chapter 7

Management of Volunteer-Based Programs

INTRODUCTION

In Chapter 3, a distinction was made between administration and guidance. The purpose of guidance, according to the distinction, is to enhance the motivation of volunteers while increasing their productivity. The goal of administration is similar: to facilitate a productive working environment. The difference lies in the nature of the activities. Those which directly affect the motivation of volunteers are guidance activities. Those which do not directly affect volunteers, such as budget and linkage development, are administrative activities. While it is true that many guidance activities are also administrative activities, such as supervision and recognition, administrative activities are seldom guidance activities.

The purpose of this chapter is to present ten managerial considerations or actions which a volunteer coordinator must address in attempting to develop an effective volunteer-based program. The first five—"Budgeting and Finance," "Managing Time," "Effectively Utilizing Records and Reports," "Establishing Community Linkages," and "Using an Advisory Committee"—can be viewed as administrative (as opposed to guidance) functions because they do not necessarily involve volunteers. Following the administrative functions are five guidance functions: "Understanding Why People Become Volunteers," "Controlling the Quality of Volunteer Performance," "Delegating Tasks," "Giving Recognition to the Volunteers' Accomplishments," and "Resolving Conflict." In addition to being guidance activities, they are also supervisory in nature because each is concerned with the execution of volunteer responsibilities.

An underlying theme of this chapter might well be the promotion of effective communication, for the establishment and maintenance of open lines of communication are important elements in each managerial activity. Volunteer coordinators are pivotal figures in this sense, initiating and overseeing the flow of information to clients, volunteers, paid staff, higher-level decision makers, funding officers, cooperative organization personnel, and the community at large. Perhaps the eventual success of a volunteer-based program rests largely upon the ability of a volunteer coordinator to communicate effectively.

ADMINISTRATIVE FUNCTIONS

Budgeting and Finance

Although volunteers work without pay, direct and indirect costs arise in any program that incorporates their services. Direct costs such as telephone expenses, meals, and travel allowances increase with each volunteer. Indirect costs for extra heating and lighting, management and supervision, and evaluation can be considerable.

Figure 7-1 shows budget items in a setting where ten volunteers work 2 hours per week tutoring adults in a literacy program. This assumes that volunteers were recruited, interviewed, trained in an 18-hour workshop, given materials to work with, and supervised and evaluated for a period of 1 year. No volunteer coordinator was hired; instead, a salaried administrator managed the program. Due to variances in specific costs among programs, budget items are presented in percentages of the total budget. While the budget contains such ancillary items as child care, travel, and tuition reimbursement, it would still be of considerable size even without them. Nevertheless, it remains true that volunteer help can provide instruction at a fraction of normal cost.

There can be no set rule governing the amount of money to be allocated for volunteers in a program, especially given the diversity of organizational goals, training programs, and management styles. However, in forecasting a budget, some fixed items, or those which are not dependent upon the number of volunteers, can be distinguished from variable items, or those which change according to the number of volunteers. An exam-

Budget item	Fixed items	Variable items	Direct costs	Indirect costs	Percentage of budget
Recruitment (newspaper advertisements, posters)	X		X		4
Interview (18 candidates, ½ hour each)		X		X	0
Preservice training (registration fees and materials)		X	X		8
Preservice training lunch		X	X		4
Instructional materials (4 books per volunteer)		X	X		10
Supervision and evaluation (1 hour per volunteer per week)		X	X		25
In-service training (registration fees and materials)		X	X		8
In-service training lunch		X	X		4
Travel		X	X		7
Postage (200 pieces of correspondence)		X	X		7
Secretarial assistance (200 hours)		X		X	0
Telephone		X		X	0
Tuition and workshop reimbursement		X	X		8
Child care		X	X		8
Heating, air conditioning, and lighting	X			X	0
Recognition ceremony		X	X		7
					100

Figure 7-1 Sample budget of volunteer-based program.

ple of a fixed cost is a consultant's fee, which remains the same if the group numbers five or twenty-five.

A closer look at Figure 7-1 reveals that most costs decline in proportion to the number of volunteers; for example, the number of books purchased, the number of miles traveled, and the number of letters typed and mailed depend upon the number of volunteers. Two items that remain relatively fixed pertain to recruitment—heating and air conditioning and lighting (a major indirect cost).

Managing Time

In Figure 7-1, the time spent establishing a program, interviewing volunteer candidates, and orienting and training them is noted as an indirect cost. This does not mean that these services were offered free of charge.

1. Try to make decisions as quickly as possible, without vacillating or postponing them. It is helpful to distinguish between minor decisions, which should not be time-consuming, and major ones, which deserve more attention and time.
2. Do "something" with every piece of paper you touch. Answer it, file it, hand it to someone else, mail it, or destroy it. Do not just read it and put it down for later attention.
3. Persuade your boss to manage time better, so that you can improve your management of time.
4. Be specific about dates, and enter them immediately on a calendar or appointment book.
5. Schedule important activities when your concentration and energy level are at their highest.
6. Schedule routine work when your concentration and energy level are lower.
7. Increase your reading and writing skills, so that you can master reading and writing tasks quickly.
8. Be selective about the tasks you agree to do. Learn to say "No" to time-consuming tasks which bore you and from which you learn little—except, of course, when you must repay a favor.
9. Control the telephone, especially when a deadline confronts you. When a short answer is not possible, tell the party you will call back.
10. Control interruptions by suggesting another time to your caller. Sometimes hide until a task is finished.
11. Limit chit-chat and aimless puttering.
12. If possible, clear off desk each night.
13. Make a daily written plan, showing specific tasks. Use asterisks to mark important ones.
14. Work on those tasks early in the day.
15. Use a reminder system—prominent notes on your desk or an alert secretary.
16. Stick to the task at hand until it is done.
17. Create "availability hours" in which to see your supervisor and others.
18. Space dull tasks with interesting ones.
19. Reward yourself with interesting jobs or favorite diversions (e.g., watching TV).
20. Learn to use small amounts of time (e.g., half-hours) productively. You may be surprised how much progress can be made on large tasks during these periods or how many small tasks can be disposed of. (If you wait for big blocks of time, they may never come.)
21. Where possible, combine tasks to save time. For example, organize library research plans so that you can do several tasks (return books, look up a reference, reserve a book) at one time. The same principle applies to telephone calls, shopping, and so on.
22. Discover your energy and frustration levels and pace yourself realistically. If you become overly tired, much time could be lost in recovering from fatigue.
23. Divide large tasks (reading ten chapters of a book in a week) into smaller ones and allocate definite times for them (two chapters on Tuesday between 2:00 and 4:00 P.M., one chapter on Thursday at 8:30 A.M.).

Figure 7-2 How to manage time better. *(Adapted from a paper presented by Jolene Scriven, assistant professor of business education, at the Adult Continuing Education Administrators Workshop, Northern Illinois University, Summer 1977.)*

It simply means that the costs were not included in the volunteer budget. The point is that, in some situations, salaried administrators will be assigned these and other responsibilities associated with a volunteer-based program, often without additional remuneration. The situation may create a shortage of time or, more accurately stated, an overload of responsibilities. As the number of volunteers grows, a supervisor is increasingly distracted from other responsibilities until, at a certain point, it seems prudent to hire a volunteer coordinator. Other solutions to the time problem include using volunteers as middle managers or increasing salaried persons' efficiency. Utilizing volunteers as middle managers, because of its applicability to a variety of situations, has been included under "Delegation" in this chapter.

Increasing efficiency has strong implications for time management, which has been attracting much attention in management literature. As Robert Mason explains, "Time, or perceived lack of it, often defeats the purposeful manager in his or her strivings for truly effective management. Managers do have control over their time. . . ."[1]

By becoming aware of how time is utilized, assigning priorities to responsibilities, eliminating time wasters, and planning on a daily, weekly, and monthly basis, managers are likely to learn how to manage their time effectively. Guidelines for time management are presented in Figure 7-2.

Effectively Utilizing Records and Reports

Records and reports are often viewed as an unwanted, but necessary program function. They can serve a variety of purposes: providing accountability to funding sources and the sponsoring organization; maintenance of internal control; evaluation of the performance of program personnel, including volunteers, paid staff who hold supervisory positions, and a volunteer coordinator; and evaluation of program components such as selection, training, and supervision. When used for evaluation purposes, the criteria to be recorded should be planned in advance of the commencement of program activities. When records are used for other purposes, it is helpful to know who will receive them and for what reason. It is also helpful to know who will be responsible for recording and storing information. Some sources of useful information are listed in Figure 7-3, along with indications of how the information may be used.

Establishing Community Linkages

Volunteer-based programs cannot exist in isolation. To find sources of volunteers, to influence a community in positive ways, and to seek fund-

---

[1]Robert C. Mason, "Managerial Role and Style," in Philip D. Langerman and Douglas H. Smith, (eds.), *Managing Adult and Continuing Education Programs and Staff,* National Association for Public Continuing and Adult Education, Washington, D. C., 1979, p. 88.

Information	Use
1. Attendance records of volunteers	To help determine volunteer motivation and morale.
2. Turnover-rate records of volunteers	To help determine effectiveness or ineffectiveness of motivation techniques or job assignments.
3. Volunteer performance/achievement reports	To determine effectiveness of volunteers and accuracy of job design.
4. Volunteer satisfaction reports	To help determine strengths and weaknesses of volunteers, jobs, and/or the environment, and training objectives.
5. Program planning reports	To determine and evaluate program objectives.
6. Job descriptions	To establish selection and training criteria.
7. Recommendations from paid staff	To evaluate and improve paid staff and volunteer relationships.
8. Recruitment information and records	To evaluate recruitment techniques and sources of volunteers.
9. Interview records	To determine suitability of candidates and to improve interview practices.
10. Selection agreements	To establish employment agreements with volunteers and to improve selection process.
11. Placement reports	To evaluate adequacy of placements.
12. In-service training evaluations	To improve subsequent training events.
13. Supervision reports	To determine performance and motivation of volunteers.
14. Management reports	To improve management practices.
15. Recognition reports	To serve as basis for recommending volunteers.
16. Community linkage reports	To maintain and strengthen community linkages.
17. Budget reports	To help in effective fiscal management, plus accurate accountability to sponsors.

Figure 7-3 Selected types of information sought for record keeping.

ing, a volunteer coordinator must have knowledge of a community. In Chapter 5, the point was made that as such knowledge increases, the task of identifying sources of volunteers becomes easier. Similarly, an understanding of the institutions within a community enhances opportunities for cooperative agreements and joint planning to overcome community problems. Volunteer-based programs rely on a community for guidance, particularly from advisory board members. The following list suggests areas of inquiry that offer help in understanding a community:

1 *History*   When, by whom, and under what circumstances was a community founded? What are the prominent local traditions—political, social, cultural?

2 *Demographic data*   How large is the population? What is the median age? What are the racial and ethnic patterns? What has been the rate of growth or decline in recent years and what has caused it? Are young families moving into or out of the area?

3 *Socioeconomic indicators*   What is the unemployment rate? What do people do for a living? Are employment patterns shifting? What is the proportion of upper, middle, and lower classes? What is the average income level, the housing situation, and the crime rate?

4 *Issues and trends*   What are the current community issues and trends? What issues and trends have arisen in the past? Which were resolved, and how?

5 *Power*   Who wields the power? Religious institutions? The press? Politicians? Industrial leaders?

6 *Politics*   What is the nature of local politics? How does the community vote? What is its political history? What are the ages of political leaders? Are they long-entrenched leaders or relatively new ones?

7 *Business and industry*   What industrial patterns exist? Are business and industry moving into the area or leaving it?

8 *Public education institutions*   How many schools, colleges, and universities are in a community? How recently were they built? Have any schools closed down? What is the situation in regard to integration of schools? What is the dropout rate? What are the educational needs of the community? What kinds of adult education programs exist in the community? What special services (counseling, special education, industrial arts, and so on) do educational institutions offer?

9 *Service organizations*   What kinds of service organizations exist? How many members do they have? What functions do they serve? How well are they utilized?

Although this list is not exhaustive, it does provide a starting point for understanding a community. Much of the information is a matter of public record and can be obtained from the public library, the archives, or the local newspaper. Other sources are public officials, newspaper editors, doctors, priests, workers, owners of businesses, and politicians.

In establishing community linkages, it is vital for a community, in turn, to understand an organization—its mission, goals, and objectives (see Chapter 2). Otherwise, misrepresentations might arise and nullify attempts to establish a good public image within a community.

Using an Advisory Board

One of the best forms of linkages between an organization and the community is the advisory board. The formation of an advisory board should be carefully considered as to representation. A preferred view is that members of an advisory board should represent many community groups. It is not uncommon for a volunteer coordinator to preplan the functions of an advisory board. As a voluntary group, it is important that members of the advisory board understand their role through an orientation to the agency or the organization. The operation of the advisory board is dependent on determining purposes, deciding membership, and planning meetings.

Determining Purposes   A primary function of an advisory board is to advise and counsel the administration and paid staff associated with a volunteer-based program. Depending on the authority vested with the advisory board, this function may be achieved in a number of ways, such as providing information and offering support to the administration, or planning, implementing, and maintaining program components. The following list is representative of specific functions of an advisory board:

1 To provide a communication linkage between a program and a community.
2 To assist in the development or review of a program philosophy and mission statement.
3 To develop or review the goals and objectives of a program.
4 To make recommendations regarding sufficient funding levels.
5 To advise in the formulation of a fund-raising strategy.
6 To provide criticism of the volunteer selection criteria.
7 To promote the program.
8 To support the volunteer recruitment efforts.
9 To offer advice concerning the adequacy and appropriateness of materials and facilities.
10 To establish or review support service objectives, e.g., the scope of child care and transportation programs.
11 To recommend criteria for program evaluation.
12 To aid in the continuous review of a program.
13 To design the volunteer recognition activities.

Thus, the specific functions of an advisory board can include a broad scope of activities. Whether determined by the volunteer coordinator, higher-level administrators, or by the board itself, well-stated purposes provide focus to a board.

Deciding on Membership   Policies regarding board membership might incorporate such aspects as size, criteria for the selection of members, the term of membership, and delegation of responsibilities. Appropriate policies need not be lengthy or complex, as the following list suggests:

1 The advisory board will have a workable size, between twelve and fifteen members.
2 Members will be chosen from among the following groups: students, volunteers, paid staff, health and welfare organizations, clergy,

business, industry, community action organizations, unions, government, neighborhood councils, and universities. An equally balanced representation will be sought.

3   Members will have an interest in volunteer-based programs, a working knowledge of the community, a willingness to contribute time, and an ability to express convictions in a group setting.

4   Members will serve for 3 years. Each year a third of the committee members will relinquish their responsibilities, enabling new members to begin a 3-year term.

5   Any member of the advisory board may recommend persons for membership. Once all nominations are made, a vote will then be taken to determine which person(s) will fill the vacant board position(s).

6   When an unexpected vacancy occurs, nominations from the board will be held at the subsequent meeting.

7   If a board member fails to attend three consecutive board meetings without extraordinary extenuating circumstances, he or she will be requested to resign.

8   A chairperson will be elected at the first meeting of every year.

9   A secretary will be elected at the first meeting of every year.

10   The chairperson and volunteer coordinator will recommend a listing of task forces based on program needs, and present the listing to the board at the second meeting for approval or modifications.

11   Board members may volunteer to serve on one or more task forces.

12   Task forces will meet as often as deemed necessary by the task force members.

13   An annual review of the task forces will occur to determine their effectiveness.

It is not to be inferred that the above policies are applicable to every advisory board. Rather, the list is intended to demonstrate the scope of policies which any advisory board must consider.

Planning Meetings   The initial meeting is crucial for building and maintaining interest among members. When well conducted, the first meeting provides a new member with a sense of purpose as well as needed information. Owing to members' varied backgrounds, a chairperson not only must create a climate which encourages participation but also must maintain and control an agenda. To accomplish a balance of control and free expression of views requires preplanning by the chairperson. Specifically, he or she must seek to achieve an open climate, decide upon length and frequency of meetings in light of the work to be accomplished, select the optimum day and time, and conduct the meeting in an efficient manner. Some suggestions to ensure more productive meetings follow:

1   An agenda prepared and delivered to board members several days in advance of a meeting allows for forethought.

2   Reminding members the day before a meeting helps to ensure high attendance.

3   Establishing a consistent schedule of meetings, e.g., every second Tuesday of each of the next 12 months, fosters high attendance.

4   While structure is preferred, a danger lies in overstructure. Meetings should include time for general discussion and summarization.

The skill of the chairperson will determine the effectiveness of an advisory board. In addition to presiding over meetings, he or she directs the agenda and spearheads the establishment of task forces. An effective chairperson often provides relevant information to members, seeks to determine a comfortable level of responsibility for each member, and oversees the development of reports and documents.

GUIDANCE FUNCTIONS

Understanding Why People Become Volunteers

Why do people volunteer? Why do some people remain volunteers and other withdraw? How can volunteer coordinators design program activities which appeal to the motives of volunteers and help to accommodate their needs and ambitions? In response to these questions, some current literature and research on the subject of human motivation will be reviewed. It is assumed that volunteer coordinators and others who design volunteer-based programs have an obligation to discover the motivations of volunteers and to recognize their needs when designing program activities.

In Chapter 4, three managerial assumptions about volunteers were explored: the calculative, participatory, and self-actualizing volunteers. The purpose was to show the relationship between those assumptions and the types of leadership patterns which emerge. It was maintained that no one assumption could be applied to all volunteers, because their needs are variable, complex, and dependent upon the different situations in which they find themselves. To help broaden this view, and to substantiate the claims that have been made, some theories of motivation will be examined.

J. R. Kidd made a distinction between intrinsic and extrinsic motives. Intrinsic motives are those which prompt a person to act for the "sake of the activity,"[3] such as the pleasures gained from the act of volunteering, the chance to utilize special skills, or something to do. Extrinsic

[3]J. R. Kidd, *How Adults Learn,* Association Press, New York, 1977, p. 103.

motives refer to an end result, "the value associated with the activity,"[4] such as gaining recognition or finding employment as a result of volunteering.

Frederick Herzberg provides another view of motivation by contrasting two sets of factors, called motivation and hygiene (maintenance). Motivation factors, which include achievement, recognition, the work itself, responsibility, advancement, and growth, produce in workers a high level of satisfaction. Hygiene (maintenance) factors, on the other hand, are potential sources of discontent. They include company policy and administration, supervision, relationships with supervisors and others, working conditions, salary, status, and security. Herzberg asserts that where workers concentrate on these maintenance factors, they tend to demonstrate little interest in the job or in the quality of their work.[5]

To return to the original question, "Why do people volunteer?" Knowles asserts that people are generally motivated by a need for growth and a related need for new experiences.[6] Growth needs refer to learning, development, and a striving to reach full potential. This view corresponds with current thinking in the area of human development, notably the belief that a person's growth continues throughout life. The need for new experiences is tantamount to the thirst for adventure and the urge to try new activities and take risks.

A study conducted by the U. S. Census Bureau sought to determine specific reasons why people volunteer.[7] The findings, which present a contrast between responses received in 1965 and 1974, appear in Figure 7-4. The total amount exceeds 100 percent because respondents were permitted to answer more than one item.

In researching the motives of volunteers in a variety of child-oriented settings, James L. Lewis discovered eleven categories:[8]

1 *Recognition* Achieving through others' extrinsic rewards.

2 *Skill maintenance* Particularly expressed by individuals who had temporarily left paid employment.

3 *Social needs* As expressed by interpersonal interaction, group identity, personal reinforcement and feedback.

[4]Ibid.

[5]Saul Gellerman, *Motivation and Productivity,* American Management Association, New York, 1963. See also George H. Litwin and Robert A. Stringer, Jr., *Motivation and Organizational Climate,* Harvard University Press, Cambridge, Mass., 1968, p. 8.

[6]Malcolm Knowles, *The Modern Practice of Adult Education: Andragogy versus Pedagogy,* Association Press, New York, 1973, p. 85.

[7]*Americans Volunteer,* ACTION (The Agency for Volunteer Service), Washington, D.C., 1975, p. 12.

[8]James L. Lewis, letter quoted in Virginia C. Patterson, "Characteristics and Motivational Factors of Volunteer Club Leaders in Evangelical Churches: An Analysis of Pioneer Girls' Club Leaders," unpublished doctoral dissertation, Northern Illinois University, 1978, pp. 24–26.

Reasons	Years	
	1965	1974
Wanted to help people	37%	53%
Enjoyed volunteer work	30%	36%
Had a sense of duty	33%	32%
Had a child in program	22%	22%
Could not refuse	6%	15%
Had nothing else to do	4%	4%
Hoped activity would lead to a paying job	3%	3%

Figure 7-4 Reasons for volunteering.

4 *Expectations of others* As a result of peer pressure, community pressure, influence of children or others.

5 *Knowledge for its own sake* Learning as opposed to skill maintenance.

6 *Loyalty to a cause* Volunteering because of a belief in the purposes of an organization.

7 *Debt repayment* Showing a desire to repay by helping others have similar experiences.

8 *Martyr syndrome* Having a desire to draw attention to sacrifices through volunteer work.

9 *Selfless desire to serve* Demonstrating a sense of putting goals of an organization above self.

10 *Volunteering for credit* Earning credit from universities, colleges, or high schools.

11 *Career rehearsal* Preparing for employment.

Lewis's research is notable for two conclusions: (1) that all volunteers interviewed had multiple reasons for volunteering and (2) that motives changed through time. Patterson's research, conducted in a religious setting, supports Lewis's conclusions.[9]

Eva Schindler-Rainman and Ronald Lippitt offer a rather specific explanation of what keeps volunteers motivated, based on Kurt Lewin's model for motivation:

1 A major motivating factor for volunteers is the opportunity to participate in problem solving and significant decision making.

2 The placement of volunteers should include some process for relating the type of work and situation to their particular interests, needs, and motivations.

3 To increase motivation, most volunteer opportunities should pro-

[9]Ibid.

vide for both self-actualizing personal development and meaningful service to the needs of others. In other words, the opportunities for volunteer service should be presented both as continuing educational opportunities to learn and grow and as opportunities to contribute one's "tithe" of much-needed social service.

4 The "contract" between the volunteer and the organization should legitimize a feasible level of commitment and allow for personal variations in time, energy, and interest without guilt or tension about divided loyalties and limited energy.

5 The on-the-job experience of the volunteer should include continuing opportunities for reflective study and evaluation and for joint planning and design of service goals and action. Much of the volunteer's sustaining and renewing motivation comes from seeing clear steps toward the group's goals and from successfully completing them one by one.

6 Needs can be met and motivation sustained more effectively if the work situation also allows for individual advancement through a series of steps leading to higher levels of responsibility, skill, learning, and influence.

7 For many volunteers, motivation will be increased if a record of activities is kept. This can become part of a résumé and may lead to paid work.

8 Motivation will be sustained best if there are regular mechanisms for supportive feedback from clients, coworkers, and professional leadership and for recognition from the agency and community.

9 Participation in meaningful training activities inside and outside the organization (e.g., conferences) is an important source of continuing motivation and growth.[10]

Schindler-Rainman and Lippitt's explanation is particularly helpful for relating motivation and retention to the design of specific program activities, especially delegating, decision making, placement, providing challenging tasks, establishment of an agreement, arranging opportunities for growth, allowing job expansion or job rotation to occur, maintenance of accurate records, fostering of supportive communication patterns, and providing training.

In conclusion, volunteers seem to be motivated by a commitment to get a job done, a desire to make a worthwhile contribution, pride in an organization, and membership, or a sense of belonging to it. Some motives can be induced, others simply maintained. Because of the wide variation of motives, a perceptive volunteer coordinator will provide a setting conducive to accommodating volunteers' needs by allowing much latitude in the design of program activities.

[10]Adapted from Eva Schindler-Rainman and Ronald Lippitt, *The Volunteer Community*, NTL Learning Resources Corporation, Fairfax, Va., 1975, p. 47.

Controlling the Quality of Volunteer Performance

Controlling is a managerial function which helps to ensure the satisfactory completion of program objectives. An essential aspect of controlling is the measurement of volunteer performance, a periodic evaluation designed to determine whether the stated program objectives are being met. When discrepancies between program objectives and actual performance exist, or when a program is not functioning properly, a manager (probably a volunteer coordinator) takes corrective action in a number of ways. Objectives may be modified, the number of volunteers may be increased or decreased, job descriptions may be modified, standards for selection and training may be altered, or new leadership patterns may be chosen. Some of these steps are formal; others are informal, such as budget changes and conferences with volunteers about their employment agreements or about delegating responsibilities.

As a process, controlling involves three elements:

1 Establishing criteria of success, standards of performance, and program objectives such as the job description and the volunteer employment agreement.

2 Measuring actual volunteer performance with respect to these stated criteria of success through observation, conferences, or formal evaluation,

3 Correcting any deviations through managerial action.[11]

To illustrate the controlling process, let us choose the example of a volunteer metropolitan citizenship council. One purpose of this group is to honor newly naturalized citizens at receptions which immediately follow citizenship ceremonies. The receptions feature a short education program, singing, and refreshments. Volunteers not only facilitate the program agenda but are also responsible for ushering the new citizens from the courthouse to the reception room. In accordance with the first point above, one objective is to persuade as many of the new citizens as possible to attend the reception. A corresponding criterion for success might be to attract 70 percent of the guests of honor. To measure the effectiveness of volunteer performance, as suggested in the second point above, one need only observe the volunteers in action. Are they reaching all who exit from the courtroom? Are the new citizens greeted with cordial invitations? Do they respond affirmatively? The crucial performance measure, of course, is the percentage of new citizens attending the reception. If participation is low, the volunteer coordinator has at least four courses of action to meet the third point above: (1) to ask the new citizens why they decided to attend or not to attend, (2) to increase the number of volun-

---

[11]Adapted from Robert C. Mason, op. cit., p. 61.

teers, (3) to ask the volunteers what to do, and (4) to lower the criteria for success. Clearly, the nature of any controlling process is dependent upon the nature of the program, types of climate, roles of volunteers, and the leadership style of the volunteer coordinator.

Delegating Tasks

In a previous section, delegation of tasks was referred to as a means of lifting a burden from overcommitted volunteer coordinators or others assuming that role. Delegation involves a transfer of authority and/or decision-making responsibilities. It can also be viewed as an important managerial activity which provides motivation akin to job promotion for volunteers. The smooth functioning of a volunteer-based program requires more than a charismatic leader or a coordinator who is willing to work long hours. It requires a person who recognizes that delegation is a viable managerial option for achieving organizational goals. Symptoms which point to a lack of delegation are as follows:[12]

1　Detailed planning accomplished at high levels.
2　High frequency of orders issued from above.
3　Limited control of management over subordinates.
4　Lack of policy or too much policy.
5　Clear evidence of overcontrol or undercontrol by the manager.
6　Undue delays in decision making through the manager's inability to reach decisions.
7　Holding back on using authority.
8　Constant criticism of staff by the manager.
9　Manager quoted frequently to justify unpopular or questionable actions.
10　Manager continually takes work home at night.

Volunteer coordinators who display a reluctance to delegate tasks often manifest fear that tasks will not be performed promptly or accurately, or they find it irksome to instruct others to perform tasks. Even at its best, delegation must make allowances for mistakes. Volunteer coordinators who delegate effectively tend to be more interested in the means by which they are achieved than in the results. In that case, delegation is facilitated, but not governed, by a management-by-objectives approach, which requires defining goals or standards of performance.

Some possible areas of delegation can be found by examining program activities. Are the recruitment and public relations campaigns effective? Is training frequent enough? Are volunteers being supervised adequately? Wilson believes that the delegation of whole areas of

[12]Ibid., p. 59.

responsibility provides more motivation to volunteers than the delegation of bits and pieces.[13] Volunteers who no longer find fulfillment in their roles may welcome an expansive approach to delegation. (Incidentally, it may prove advantageous to volunteer coordinators to delegate tasks which they like, not those which they dislike, because supervision could be easier.) Sources of volunteers for middle management positions may be sought within the ranks, either as an expansion of a current role or as a transfer to a new role. Or new volunteers may be sought through advertisements. Either way, it is wise to regard the position of these middle management volunteers as similar to the positions of other volunteers with regard to the selection, training, and supervision processes. A volunteer coordinator should pay careful attention to maintaining the role of middle manager and supporting the volunteer who holds that role. The following procedures may be instructive:

1 Establish a job description, complete with areas of responsibility.
2 Develop selection guidelines.
3 Involve volunteers and paid staff in the selection decision.
4 Provide a thorough orientation to the volunteer.
5 Provide training for a volunteer in the area of involvement.
6 Delegate authority to accomplish the goals.
7 Maintain open channels of communication.
8 Provide support and assist in planning efforts.
9 Meet regularly.
10 Evaluate progress regularly.
11 Recognize a volunteer's efforts.

Delegation of tasks will not eliminate a volunteer coordinator's work, but it can be expected to change the nature of the work. Obviously, supervision of a middle management volunteer would be needed, and a coordinator would enjoy somewhat less contact with the program.

Giving Recognition to the Volunteers' Accomplishments

The Lewis study cited above lists recognition as a motivation factor for volunteers. For that reason, it is viewed as a guidance function. Recognition is a personal, honest acknowledgment of the efforts of a volunteer by a volunteer coordinator and/or others associated with a program. Although most of them would agree as to its importance, great diversity exists in the ways it is implemented. Some techniques involve public recognition, others private. Some techniques are planned celebrations, others

[13]Marlene Wilson, *The Effective Management of Volunteer Programs,* Volunteer Management Associates, Boulder, Colo., 1977, pp. 32–34.

	Public recognition	Private recognition
Planned events	Awards ceremonies, public receptions and banquets Cooperative interagency recognition events Citations for outstanding service Pins, gifts, or symbols of achievement Invite press to events Edit a recognition edition of the agency newsletter	Send letter to volunteer's placement file Send note and/or flowers to spouse of volunteer Recommend volunteer to prospective employer Present volunteer with small gifts (for example, subscription to a newspaper or journal)
Spontaneous events	Nominate for civic or organizational awards Send articles to newspapers regularly	Getting to know volunteers well Meetings with volunteers to discuss their needs, strengths, and weaknesses Attitude of respect to volunteers Utilize volunteers as consultants Encourage administrative personnel to socialize with volunteers Invite volunteers to staff meetings Offer special privileges to volunteers such as use of desk, office, or special bus

Figure 7-5   Recognition techniques.

spontaneous. Figure 7-5 shows a partial listing of recognition techniques. Sincerity demands that the techniques chosen should acknowledge the nature of a volunteer's contribution to an organization.

Resolving Conflict

The purpose of this section is to identify selected interorganizational and intraorganizational conflicts which can prove dysfunctional to the purposes and operation of an organization and to present recommendations for resolving these conflicts. The starting point will be a listing of roadblocks to communication which frequently underlie such conflicts. Attention will then be given to resolving conflicts between a volunteer coordinator and paid staff and between a coordinator and higher-level decision makers. Lastly, conflicts which surround voluntarism as an enterprise and which may impinge on programs will be explored.

Some roadblocks to communication which can prevent swift and just resolution of conflicts appear on the following page:[14]

[14]Adapted from Marlene Wilson, op. cit., pp. 172–173.

   1 *Inaccessibility*   When a leader is remote from a situation, physically or psychologically, communication and the development of healthy relationships become virtually impossible. Volunteers are likely to feel keenly the inaccessibility of volunteer coordinators and other officials.
   2 *Distortion*   Distortion of information accidently and/or deliberately engenders confusion because it offends people's cherished beliefs.
   3 *Lack of trust*   Lack of trust induces people to withhold opinions that are negative or critical. Fearing what they perceive as an inherent risk, they tend to "play it safe."
   4 *Hidden agendas*   Entry into a relationship with a hidden, predetermined, and manipulative motive will reduce trust in the long run.
   5 *Ineffective listening*   Ineffective listening often represents a desire to dominate, accompanied by unwillingness to tolerate others' views. It may cause a person to interrupt frequently.
   6 *Formulating conclusions prematurely*   Failure to keep an open mind until all arguments have been examined causes people to jump to conclusions. This tendency may represent a wish to force a desired conclusion.
   7 *Belief in absolutes*   This behavior involves relying on generalizations or prejudices in forming opinions and may lead to a tendency to cast blame.
   8 *Right-and-wrong syndrome*   This entails a belief that only two sides of an issue exist, an attitude that may preclude compromise.
   9 *Traditional beliefs*   Time-honored beliefs often cause a tendency in a person to seek singular answers to problems.
   10 *Individual differences*   Allowing differences of race, age, or status to predominate makes it difficult to appreciate others' points of view.

   One major challenge for a volunteer coordinator is to prevent conflict between paid staff and volunteers. Problems involving threats to status, fear of losing a job, and misunderstandings can lead paid staff to compete, not collaborate, with volunteers. It is a coordinator's responsibility to establish channels of communication and cooperative agreements. As discussed in Chapter 3, one way of doing so is to involve paid staff in the volunteer program and to show them how volunteers might actually relieve some of their job pressures. Paid staff can be involved in numerous ways: in the program design phase, selection process, training activities, supervision process, and evaluation process. Once good relationships have been established, certain measures can be taken by a volunteer coordinator to maintain them:

   1 Emphasize the importance of productivity of the entire organization and recognize every person's contribution.
   2 Inform paid staff of the philosophy and goals of a volunteer-based program.

3 Inform volunteers of the paid staff's authority.

4 Create opportunities for everyone to ventilate concerns honestly and openly.

5 Recognize that conflict can be used for identifying needed areas of change.

6 Be supportive, not defensive, toward attempts to examine problems.

7 Seek advice from paid staff and be willing to accept and respond to that advice.

8 Make certain that cooperative agreements and areas of involvement are understood by volunteers and paid staff alike.

Overcoming Opposition to Volunteers

At times, a sponsoring organization may not be supportive of a volunteer-based program and may not provide a setting which will encourage its growth. In that case, a coordinator may be called upon to correct the misconceptions of antivolunteer administrators and to address their specific concerns. Knowles identifies three strategies for coping with this type of situation: (1) seek to change the larger organization and to educate its officials; (2) develop a semiautonomous organization within the larger organization, thus lessening mutual dependencies; or (3) negotiate gradual modifications in policies to allow a volunteer-based program to become increasingly autonomous.[15]

In regard to top-level administrators, Ivan Scheirer describes three types: (1) those visibly and vocally opposed to volunteers, (2) those who are unrealistically enthusiastic, and (3) those who offer passive support.[16] For administrators who oppose voluntary efforts, as well as those who are overly enthusiastic, the following recommendations apply:

1 Encourage them to visit successful volunteer-based programs or to accept visitors from successful programs.

2 Involve them in volunteer activities within and without an organization.

3 Inform them of endorsements from others.

4 Keep them apprised of the progress of the program.

For administrators who offer passive support, the following recommendations apply:

1 Make them aware of the amount of time, expertise, and money available to conduct a volunteer-based program.

[15]Malcolm Knowles, op. cit., p. 63.

[16]Ivan Scheirer, *Orienting Paid Staff to Volunteers,* National Information Center on Voluntarism, Boulder, Colo., 1972, p. 36.

2   Explain the nature of the contribution they would be asked to make to a volunteer-based program.

3   Acquaint them with the potential benefits to themselves.

Opposition to volunteer-based programs exists outside of an organization as well. According to Schindler-Rainman and Lippitt, two such sources are women's groups and unions.[17] Women's groups, particularly the National Organization for Women, aim their criticism of voluntarism primarily at service groups, claiming that such activities degrade women and prevent them from entering the work force. Unions see in the vast potential of the voluntarism movement a danger that volunteers will be used as an excuse to take away jobs or reduce budgets. But Schindler-Rainman and Lippitt insist that "it is not the purpose of the volunteer movement in the United States to take paid work away from anyone."[18]

Upon closer examination, critics might discover that volunteering is a way for people to become fulfilled and that a decision to volunteer is individual and personal. Furthermore, if present trends hold, volunteer programs will increasingly attract both men and women, even though greater numbers of women are expected to enter the work force. As the voluntarism movement grows in stature and professionalism, criticisms will probably diminish.

CONCLUSION

The considerations and actions that have been discussed inevitably create a view of the kind of leadership required in volunteer settings. The discussion augments the view presented in the concluding remarks of Chapter 3 concerning the multifaceted aspect of the role of a volunteer coordinator. It is a pivotal role whose responsibilities extend to many distinct groups of people within and outside an organization. Perhaps the most difficult aspect of the role is to confront skeptical members of an organization who are reluctant to participate in a volunteer-based program. To a great extent, a volunteer coordinator's command of administrative and guidance skills will prove to be the crucial factor in launching such a program and maintaining its viability. Special importance is attached to communication skills, which include sensitivity to others's needs and a realization that his or her leadership style will affect others' behavior, a propensity to quickly detect and break down barriers to effective communication, and an ability to manage conflicts.

[17]Eva Schindler-Rainman and Ronald Lippitt, op. cit., pp. 44–45.
[18]Ibid.

Chapter 8

Evaluation of Volunteer-Based Programs

INTRODUCTION

The purpose of this chapter is to explore the nature and practical application of volunteer-based program evaluation. To achieve this purpose, the following topics will be addressed: the meaning of evaluation, what to evaluate, points of evaluation, who should evaluate, selecting methods of evaluation, and frequent problems with evaluation, including an examination of basic assumptions and misapprehensions.

MEANING OF EVALUATION

In attempting to define "evaluation," its nature and purpose, it is useful to examine several definitions. One definition reads:

> . . . a process by which evidence, criteria and judgments are used in managing resources and facilitating accurate and appropriate decision making in areas of major importance. . .[1]

[1]Sara Steele, "Program Evaluation as an Administrative Concept," paper delivered at AERA Annual Meeting, New Orleans, Feb. 28, 1973, p. 8.

Evaluation, then, is a strategy which enables the volunteer coordinator or other decision makers to make enlightened decisions about the distribution of program resources such as time, funds and people. Evaluation is not the exclusive domain of skilled consultants. Rather, it is a collaborative, ongoing activity that might involve many people associated with a volunteer-based program.

Another definition recognizes evaluation as a multipart activity:

> Evaluation is the determination (whether based on opinions, records, subjective or objective data) of the results (whether desirable or undesirable; transient or permanent; immediate or delayed) attained by some activity (whether a program or part of a program. . . . . an ongoing or one-shot approach) designed to accomplish some valued goal or objective (whether ultimate, intermediate, or immediate, effort or performance, long or short range). This definition contains four key dimensions: (1) Process—the "determination"; (2) Criteria—the "results"; (3) Stimulus—the "activity"; and (4) Value—the "objective." The scientific method with its accompanying research techniques then provides the most promising means for "determining" the relationship of the "stimulus" to the "objective" in terms of measurable "criteria."[2]

Evaluation is, therefore, based on a plan. Certain aspects of the plan require predetermination, such as what will be evaluated, the criteria for measurement, the methods used, and how the results will be used.

A third definition recognizes the broad nature and purpose of evaluation as

> . . . a process of examining certain objects and events in the light of specific value standards for the purpose of making adaptive decisions.[3]

The implication is that the purposes of evaluation can be very specific, especially when the standards are specific. Understanding various purposes increases the value of conducting evaluation for all concerned. The following list relates a wide variety of purposes:

1   To assess the effectiveness of program components such as planning, recruitment, and training.

2   To help determine the benefits and/or detriments of program expansion or reduction.

---

[2]Edward A. Suchman, *Evaluative Research,* Russell Sage Foundation, New York, 1967, pp. 31–32.

[3]C. F. Paulson, *A Strategy for Evaluative Design,* Teaching Research, Oregon State System of Higher Education, Monmouth, Oreg., 1970, p. 1, as used in Arden Grotelueschen et al., *Evaluation in Adult Basic Education: How and Why,* Interstate Printers and Publishers, Danville, Ill. 1976, p. 17.

3 To document successes, and consequently avoid institutional criticism.
4 To account for program expenditures.
5 To determine the appropriateness of the content area.
6 To ascertain the strengths and weaknesses of program personnel.

Clearly, there are multiple purposes, or combinations of them, for conducting an evaluation. Arden Grotelueschen believes that most of them can fit into the broad evaluative categories of past events, present events, and future events, or, as he terms it, "past activities, or outcomes; current program activities; and possible future actions."[4] The distinction is useful for pointing out the time-related differences among accountability, program improvement, and planning.

WHAT TO EVALUATE

An understanding of the purposes of evaluation and an awareness of what kind of information is required are prerequisites for determining what is to be evaluated. As an ongoing process, evaluation begins with the initial planning phase when program components such as recruitment and training are defined. Of particular importance are objectives, which should be constructed in such a way that they can be measured or observed. For example, if twelve volunteers are to be recruited to tutor non-English-speaking adults 2 hours per week for a year, measurable criteria for success may be predetermined, such as student performance on the conversational level, volunteer attendance, and the effects of training on volunteer performance. The initial design of the evaluation process provides a plan for the measurement of program components in a systematic manner.

What is evaluated, then, are program components, especially objectives. The following selective list presents such measurable program components:

1 Program design
   a Program planning
   b Job design
   c Facilities
   d Coordination with paid staff
2 Selection
   a Recruitment
   b Interview
   c Selection decision

[4]Arden Grotelueschen, "Evaluation," in a book to be published by the Adult Education Association and Jossey-Bass.

3 Socialization and Training
   a Orientation and preservice training
   b Placement
   c In-service training
4 Guidance
   a Supervision
   b Motivation
   c Recognition
5 Administration
   a Community linkages
   b Records and reports
   c Budget
   d Evaluation design

POINTS OF EVALUATION

Program components are not easily measured by themselves. It may be insufficient, for example, simply to know that a training activity has occurred. In order to produce meaningful information, the components need to be made operational and defined in measurable, action-oriented terms. Some components may be defined in terms of objectives which become the points of evaluation. For example, one objective of in-service training may be to introduce volunteers to the use of a new technique. In that instance, information would be sought regarding the utility and frequency of use of that technique. Other components that might be treated in this way are cost efficiency, anticipated results, unanticipated results, volunteer performance, student achievement, volunteer satisfaction, or turnover rate. Points of evaluation must be measurable and should be predetermined. In addition, we might ask ourselves what criteria can be used to evaluate the morale of volunteers? Absenteeism, turnover rate, and the feelings of the volunteers may come to mind. Yet, if morale was also to be measured in terms of how frequently and willingly volunteers attend training sessions, the need and provision for training would require predetermination.

Some components can be made operational according to subactivities. Recruitment, for example, suggests subactivities such as the success of public relations methods, printed materials, and the electronic media. The efforts spent formulating objectives from major goals during the planning process should also facilitate the evaluation process.

As for specific standards used to judge points of evaluation, they are usually predetermined by program personnel. Acceptable standards for measurement, or criteria for success, serve to guide an evaluation. It may be unrealistic to assume that a single acceptable standard of success exists for all agencies. Perhaps more realistic is the assumption that the specific nature of criteria for success should differ among programs. Nevertheless, as Figure 8-1 shows, it is possible to view program components in terms of measurable points of evaluation.

Program components	Criteria for measurement
I. Program design	
1. Program planning	• The resulting objectives • The achievement of objectives • Adherence to objectives • Program outcomes • Satisfaction of volunteer coordinator • Satisfaction of higher level decision makers
2. Job design	• Satisfaction of students or clients • Satisfaction of volunteers • Satisfaction of volunteer coordinator • Turnover rate • Absenteeism rate • Opinion of paid staff • Number of unplaced volunteers • Number of unfilled volunteer jobs
3. Facilities	• Working environment • Storage space • Lighting • Seating • Frequency of audio and visual distractions • Cost
4. Coordination with paid staff	• Paid staff's knowledge of the purpose of the volunteer-based program • Time expended by paid staff • Level of involvement of paid staff • Adherence to written guidelines of cooperation • Volunteer's knowledge of organization
II. Selection	
5. Recruitment	• Time and effort expended • Cost • Success of promotional methods used, such as newspaper, radio, and television • Turnover rate • Sources of volunteers • Placement/nonplacement rate • Performance of volunteers • Satisfaction of volunteers
6. Interview	• Suitability of interview design or written interview guide • Qualifications of interviewers • Turnover rate • Quality and accuracy of information given to volunteer • Time spent interviewing • Opinion of volunteers

Figure 8-1 Selected criteria for measurement.

Program components	Criteria for measurement
7. The selection decision	• Number of volunteers accepted • Number of volunteers refused • Terms of volunteer agreement • Criteria for selection • Agreement and adherence to termination date • Turnover rate
III. Socialization and training	
8. Orientation and preservice training	• Assimilation process for new volunteers • Degree and evidence of teamwork, group cohesiveness, and democratic process • Methods and techniques used • Resources expended • Evidence that skills, attitudes, or knowledge learned is appropriate to the job • Volunteer motivation and enthusiasm • Opinions of paid staff • Nature of information available to the volunteer
9. Placement	• Choices offered volunteers • Turnover rate • Criteria used for placement • Satisfaction of volunteers • Satisfaction of paid staff
10. In-service training	• Frequency and duration • Resources expended • Evidence that learning occurs • Methods and techniques used • Interest level • Attitude of volunteers • Turnover rate • Evaluation of training sessions • Volunteer performance • Evidence that skills, attitudes, and knowledge of volunteers are appropriate to the assignment • Opinion of volunteers
IV. Guidance	
11. Supervision/motivation	• Adherence to employment agreement • Evidence of sponsorship of volunteers • Motivation techniques used • Recognition techniques used • Number of reassignments • Amount of job rotation • Type of climate • Goals of volunteers • Turnover rate • Volunteer satisfaction • Group spirit • Methods of volunteer appraisal used • Communication flow • Accessibility of volunteer coordinator

Program components	Criteria for measurement
12. Management	• Type of leadership demonstrated • Nature of hierarchy • Problem-solving techniques used • Amount of delegation of responsibility • Clarity and specificity of responsibilities • Cooperation of organization • Nature of community linkages • Resources expended • Adequacy of planning • Organizational relations • Volunteers' opinion of management • Turnover rate • Dynamics of the volunteer group
13. Recognition	• Scheduled events • Opinion of volunteers • Publicity techniques used • System of rewards of incentives, i.e., certificates, pins, plaques
V. Administration 14. Community linkages	• Time and effort spent recruiting, including number of speaking engagements and joint campaigns • Types of linkages planned • Types of linkages realized • Opinion of administrative decision makers
15. Records and reports	• Type of data available • Type of data required • Purpose of records and reports • Time spent • Depth of coverage
16. Budgeting	• Proposals written • Sources of funding • Allocation of funds • Clarity of records
17. Evaluation	• Purposes • What is evaluated • Criteria chosen • Time and money spent evaluating • Frequency of evaluation • Utility of results • Reliability of results • Methods and techniques used • Evidence that results are usable • Evidence that results are shared • Evidence that results are acted upon

Figure 8-1 *(Continued, opposite and above)*

The sample listing of points of evaluation in Figure 8-1 could directly assist an evaluator in making selected program components operational. However, the main intention of such a listing is simply to demonstrate the necessity and feasibility of defining major areas of evaluation in measurable terms. Of course, certain components are more difficult to make operational than others. In evaluating the morale of a program, for example, one may never be sure that the criteria are exhaustive. However, in most cases, a little information is better than none.

To further illustrate the importance of points of evaluation, one item will be selected and made operational for each program component in Figure 8-1. Such treatment should reveal the value of predetermining points of evaluation. It is not to be assumed that each of the examples in Figure 8-2 is equally applicable to every institution or agency.

THOSE WHO SHOULD EVALUATE THE PROGRAM

Involving a variety of people in the evaluation process has several advantages. First, it allows them to become more familiar with the volunteer-based program. Second, it fosters a sense of belonging and may increase morale among the paid staff. Third, a wide range of opinions from a variety of vantage points often leads to a more valid evaluation. The comments given below relate to the different groups that should be involved in the evaluation process.

Volunteers

If we want to know what volunteers experience, how they feel, what their motivations and goals are, and what suggestions they have for program improvement, why not ask them? Their judgments are important because each individual has a unique view of the program.

Paid Supervisory Staff

Paid supervisory staff directly associated with volunteers also hold specific views of the program—its trends, leadership, and potential—and may be a source of much data. A possible drawback is that competing demands and ego involvement may intrude when paid staff work with particularly capable volunteers and form a biased opinion of the program as a whole. For example, as a relationship of mutual respect develops between a volunteer and a paid staff person, the latter may lose impartiality toward a volunteer's performance.

Other Paid Staff

Although other paid staff are indirectly involved with a volunteer-based program, not with its day-to-day activities, they can add another perspective to the evaluation process by explaining how they have been affected by the program and what attitudes they hold toward volunteers.

Program components	Making points of evaluation operational
Program planning	As a point of evaluation, program outcomes, such as a well-balanced group of volunteers from the various segments of the community, are important criteria to measure the effectiveness of program planning.
Job design	A point of evaluation for job design is the number of unplaced volunteers. If it is extraordinarily high, an evaluator might recommend a review of the nature and variety of volunteer positions. Of course, agency personnel would decide how many unplaced volunteers the program could tolerate.
Facilities	An evaluation of facilities may include a determination of the adequacy of natural and artificial lighting by taking into account the opinions of volunteers and clients.
Coordination with paid staff	A helpful point often used to evaluate coordination with paid staff is the time expended by paid staff with volunteers, especially if thought to be insufficient. If this is the case, a volunteer coordinator would be advised to consider the extent of social interaction.
Recruitment	One important point in evaluating recruitment is the successful use of promotional media such as newspapers, radio, and television. A measure of a program's success may be found by comparing predetermined objectives with actual outcomes. For example, if an objective of a radio advertisement is to recruit fifty listeners and only two enroll, then it would appear that the radio advertisement is not effective in reaching prospective volunteers.
Interview	An evaluation of the interview process might include measuring the turnover rate and scrutinizing its fluctuations over time. What constitutes an acceptable turnover rate will vary from program to program. Undoubtedly, the quality of the interview process has much to do with turnover rate.
The selection decision	Measuring the number of volunteers accepted is one example of a point of evaluation. If the number of volunteers accepted into a program falls short of expectations, this would indicate that the selection criteria need further examination.
Orientation and preservice training	Evidence that skills, attitudes, and knowledge learned is appropriate to the job can be measured by observing participants in their work to determine if the content of training sessions is being applied. If not, the reasons for this inadequacy should be sought from the volunteers.

Figure 8-2 Making points of evaluation operational.

Program components	Making points of evaluation operational
Placement	As a point of evaluation, satisfaction of volunteers can be elicited, revealing the degree to which they enjoy their work. Subsequent evaluations may provide additional insights into volunteer satisfaction.
In-service training	One point that might be used to evaluate in-service training is the success of the training sessions, which may be measured by assessing participant satisfaction.
Supervision/motivation	The rate of job rotation is a popular point of evaluation when assessing morale. The frequent use of job rotation as a managerial technique indicates that serious attempts are being made to increase morale.
Management	A measurable point of evaluating management is assessing appropriateness of the type of leadership demonstrated. An evaluator may seek to understand the opinions of volunteers regarding the leadership of the volunteer coordinator.
Recognition	One point of evaluation is the appropriateness of the system of rewards and incentives, such as certificates, pins, and plaques. By carefully surveying volunteers, an evaluator gains important information regarding recognition.
Community linkages	Types of linkages realized, or the number and nature of agreements made between the volunteer program and other community agencies, can be confirmed simply by asking the volunteer coordinator.
Records and reports	An examination of the time spent on records and reports is a key point of evaluation. Either too much or too little time spent on records and reports justifies the attention of an evaluator.
Budgeting	The nature and sources of funding is a significant point of evaluation. An evaluator may scrutinize the actual sources of funding and rate them according to the amount of flexibility allowed by the granting agency. It is necessary to bear in mind the period of time for which funding is made available. A continuing dependency on short-term funding diverts energies away from other aspects of a program.
Evaluation	Evaluation is an ongoing process. The very fact that the administrator acknowledges the importance of evaluation is itself a positive indicator of the quality of the program.

Figure 8-2 *(Continued)*

Volunteer Coordinator

Since the major responsibility for volunteers falls on the shoulders of a volunteer coordinator, he or she is perhaps in the best position to understand program strengths and weaknesses and to guide the implementation of evaluation. Furthermore, because a volunteer coordinator must act upon the results of an evaluation, he or she should certainly understand where the information came from and how it was obtained.

Outside Experts

Evaluation experts who are unfamiliar with a program may offer skilled methods of obtaining data and objective means for its interpretation. Consultants are commonly used in situations demanding objectivity. Disadvantages of employing consultants include the additional costs incurred and their limited knowledge of program aspects such as historical background, politics, or attitudes.

Administrative Decision Makers

Involvement of organization officials seems advantageous because it offers the possibility of building rapport with them. Although they may not be familiar with all the details of a program, their special vantage point might allow for a more holistic view that could lead to helpful judgments and subsequently to program improvement.

Community Representatives

When a volunteer program relies on community involvement and support (as it often must), representatives from the community might offer good advice in such matters as the "image" of the program, recruitment techniques, and public relations.

Advisory Board Members

As representatives of the community who possess intimate knowledge of the program, members of the advisory board might provide helpful insight concerning administrative policies, such as community linkages and public relations.

Students or Clients

Considerable importance should be attached to the opinions of students or clients—those who may be most affected by the volunteer-based program. An obvious concern relates to whether progress has been made toward achieving their goals.

As we have tried to show, there are advantages to using a variety of people in the evaluation process. Yet certain individuals are in a better position than others to evaluate some aspects of a program. The restate-

Program components	Evaluator
I. Program design	
1. Program planning	• Outside experts • Administrative decision makers • Volunteer coordinator
2. Job design	• Students or clients • Volunteers • Volunteer coordinator • Paid staff
3. Facilities	• Students or clients • Volunteers • Volunteer coordinator
4. Coordination with paid staff	• Administrative/decision makers • Volunteer coordinator • Paid staff • Volunteers
II. Selection	
5. Recruitment	• Outside expert • Volunteer coordinator • Volunteers • Community representatives
6. Interview	• Interviewer • Volunteer coordinator • Volunteers • Outside expert
7. The selection decision	• Volunteer coordinator • Volunteers
III. Socialization and training	
8. Orientation and preservice training	• Program planner • Volunteer coordinator • Presentor • Participants • Outside expert
9. Placement	• Volunteer coordinator • Paid staff • Volunteers • Students or clients
10. In-service training	• Program planner • Volunteer coordinator • Presentor • Participants • Outside expert

Figure 8-3 Who should evaluate.

Program components	Evaluator
IV. Guidance	
11. Supervision/motivation	• Volunteer coordinator
	• Volunteers
	• Paid staff
	• Outside expert
12. Management	• Administrative decision makers
	• Volunteer coordinator
	• Volunteers
	• Outside expert
13. Recognition	• Volunteer coordinator
	• Paid staff
	• Volunteers
V. Administration	
14. Community linkages	• Administrative decision makers
	• Volunteer coordinator
	• Community representatives
	• Outside expert
15. Records and reports	• Administrative decision makers
	• Volunteer coordinator
	• Volunteers
16. Budgeting	• Funding source representative
	• Volunteer coordinator
	• Administrative decision makers
17. Evaluation	• Outside expert
	• Volunteer coordinator
	• Volunteers
	• Administrative decision makers

Figure 8-3 *(Continued)*

ment of program components in Figure 8-3 is accompanied by suggestions concerning who should evaluate each component.

Figure 8-3 suggests that people will be vitally concerned with selected evaluation activities because of the nature of their involvement with the program. For example, paid staff will be most aware of program components related to their own supervisory responsibilities such as job design, coordination with paid staff, placement, and supervision motivation. The volunteer coordinator, because of his or her responsibilities to the program as a whole, would not be totally excluded from the evaluation of any program aspect. However, when objectivity is demanded, he or she may wish to assume a passive role. For higher-level decision makers who must be concerned with the well-being of the entire sponsoring organization, it is suggested that they be involved with the evaluation of such components as program planning, coordination with paid staff, management, community linkages, records and reports, budgeting, and evaluation.

WHEN TO EVALUATE

Thus far it has been suggested that evaluation be introduced during the program planning phase and continue as an ongoing activity. Of course, this does not mean that elaborate evaluation schemes should be conducted on a daily basis. Rather, the timing of evaluation depends upon what aspect of a program is being assessed and the intended uses of the results. Examples of times when evaluation should be conducted include: before reporting to a funding source, before annual program planning, following preservice or in-service training sessions, or when crises arise. Figure 8-4 shows more precisely the timing of evaluation of particular program components by associating what is to be evaluated with a time specification.

Program components	When
I. Program design	
1. Program planning	• Upon completion and continually in an informal way
2. Job design	• Annually
3. Facilities	• Annually
4. Coordination with paid staff	• Annually
II. Selection	
5. Recruitment	• Following recruitment activities
6. Interviewing	• Monthly
7. Final selection decision	• Monthly
III. Socialization and training	
8. Orientation and preservice training	• At the conclusion of sessions
9. Placement	• Monthly
10. In-service training	• At the conclusion of each session
	• Several weeks following each session
IV. Guidance	
11. Supervision/motivation	• Continually in an informal way
12. Management	• Annually
13. Recognition	• Annually
V. Administration	
14. Community linkages	• Annually or prior to establishing new linkages
15. Records and reports	• Annually
16. Budget	• Monthly or before each advisory board meeting
17. The evaluation design	• Annually

Figure 8-4 When to evaluate.

SELECTING METHODS OF EVALUATION

An impressive array of data collection techniques is available within the social sciences for the purpose of determining facts, beliefs, attitudes, standards of action, and reasons for policies and behavior. Furthermore, elaborate correlative schemes and statistical procedures can be used to judge the significance, reliability, and validity of information. The selection of such tools depends largely upon the precision demanded of the data, the type of analysis desired, and the purpose of the information. Much needed information can be found by using a few techniques such as questionnaires, interviews, the examination of records, and observation. Choices among them can be made easier by examining their advantages and disadvantages.

Questionnaires

The art of constructing valid and reliable questionnaires involves translating what needs to be measured into clear and understandable questions which can be interpreted similarly and consistently by the respondents. Such uniformity of wording helps to ensure uniformity of measurement.

Advantages of Questionnaires

1 They can be cost-efficient.
2 They provide ease of administration and tabulation.
3 Large numbers of people can be surveyed at one time.
4 They can be distributed through the mail.
5 Confidentiality can be guaranteed.

Disadvantages of Questionnaires

1 They can be burdensome to the respondent.
2 Questions may force choices and opinions.
3 The range of choices may be limited.
4 Biases may affect reliability of the questions.
5 The return rate may be low.
6 The meaning of questions may differ from person to person.
7 Questions may not address all of the important problems as perceived by respondents.

Interviews

Interviews are face-to-face encounters between an evaluator and a respondent. They may be structured or informal. In a structured interview, an evaluator uses a list of questions to guide the flow of the conversation. Skillful evaluators attract and hold the interest of respondents, while guiding them from item to item. The manner and the language of an evaluator can affect the results.

Advantages of Interviews

1 Interviews can be used for everyone involved with the program.
2 Information gained tends to be complete.
3 Flexibility exists for asking important questions.
4 An allowance can be made for probing.
5 They offer an opportunity for the information to be validated.
6 The response rate is usually high.
7 There is less chance to misinterpret a question or definition.
8 More information may be obtained from an interview than from a questionnaire.

Disadvantages of Interviews

1 Large amounts of time and money are often required.
2 A high level of expertise is needed.
3 Many factors such as attitudes, situational factors, and setting affect the results.
4 Trust must be established even though confidentiality cannot be guaranteed.
5 Interviewers' biases may affect the validity of the questions.
6 Questions may not help solve the problem.
7 The wording of questions may change from interview to interview.
8 Data may be difficult to analyze.

Program Records

If a volunteer coordinator has foresight, he or she will establish a record-keeping system that will facilitate evaluation. The task of evaluation becomes eased when access can be gained to goal statements, agreements, and other records that have been carefully maintained. Records concerning recruitment, selection criteria, placement, training, supervision, and evaluation are particularly helpful. In general, records provide useful program development information for an evaluation team to consider.

Advantages of Program Records

1 Records tend to supplement other data.
2 They are convenient.
3 They may provide a beginning for the data collection process.

Disadvantages of Program Records

1 Viewing records may not meet with the approval of all concerned.
2 Records may be difficult to interpret.
3 Definitions of terms may differ, causing misleading information.
4 Validity and reliability may be low.
5 Records may be incomplete.
6 Records may be inaccessible (Privacy Act).

Observation

Perhaps the most frequently used evaluation technique is observation. Observing reactions to training and recognition events, for example, may provide clues to a person's level of satisfaction. As a useful evaluation technique, observation is neither casual nor unplanned. A deep level of understanding of what is to be evaluated and a systematic strategy for finding and recording information are required. Furthermore, an observer must come to terms with those biases and expectations which may influence the information-gathering procedures. An observer must be well trained to be effective.

Advantages of Observation

1 An observer can be unobtrusive.
2 Unexpected results can be taken into account.
3 Interesting and useful insights about program procedures may be found.
4 More information may be obtained by observation than by an interview.

Disadvantages of Observation

1 Large amounts of time may be required.
2 Not all situations are conducive to good observation.
3 An observer cannot manipulate the data.
4 A systematized method of recording data is required.
5 It is often difficult to discern a person's true beliefs by observation.
6 An observer's biases can easily influence the quality of the results.

The selection of a data-gathering technique should take into consideration not only the type of information sought but also the source of information. For example, asking a student of adult basic education to tackle a

Program components	Methods of evaluation
I. Program design	
1. Program planning	• Interview • Records • Questionnaire • Observation
2. Job design	• Interview • Records • Questionnaire
3. Facilities	• Interview • Observation
4. Coordination with paid staff	• Interview • Records • Questionnaire
II. Selection	
5. Recruitment	• Interview • Records • Questionnaires
6. Interview	• Interview • Records
7. The selection decision	• Records
III. Socialization and training	
8. Orientation and preservice training	• Interview • Questionnaire • Observation
9. Placement	• Interview • Records
10. In-service training	• Observation • Records • Interview

Figure 8-5 Methods of evaluation.

complicated questionnaire is clearly inappropriate. Similarly, asking for the volunteer's opinions of the leadership ability of the volunteer coordinator in a group situation is inappropriate.

Figure 8-5 repeats the program components and matches them with suggested methods of evaluation.

PROBLEMS OF EVALUATION

Even the most carefully designed evaluation plan faces potential problems. For example, many important program aspects such as the climate

Program components	Methods of evaluation
IV. Guidance	
11. Supervision/motivation	• Observation • Interview • Records
12. Management	• Records • Interview • Questionnaire
13. Recognition	• Observation • Interview • Records
V. Administration	
14. Community linkages	• Records • Interview
15. Records and reports	• Records • Interview
16. Budget	• Interview • Records
17. The evaluation design	• Records • Observation • Interview

Figure 8-5   *(Continued)*

and the leadership style of the volunteer coordinator simply cannot be easily measured. In addition, it is probably true that certain unintended beneficial results of volunteer programs escape the attention of some evaluation designs. One reason is that volunteer-based programs are fluid situations, in which such variables as attitudes and values can change with unpredictable regularity and speed. Other common problems of evaluation include:

1 Lack of agreement about program goals and components.
2 Ill-defined and unmeasurable objectives.
3 Absence of a preconceived plan.
4 Lack of a purpose for evaluating.
5 Neglect of hard-to-measure aspects, such as attitudes, secondary consequences, and values.
6 Neglecting to inform people associated with the program of the intended use of results.
7 Failure to take action on the results.
8 Spending more time and money than necessary.

CONCLUSION

In this chapter, evaluation has been viewed as an ongoing strategy of gaining information for program improvement. Its achievement is usually based on a logical plan of action which includes the reasons for evaluation, determining what to evaluate, specifying the points of evaluation, deciding upon who should do evaluation, and selecting methods of evaluation. It should be recognized that the specific criteria used to judge points of evaluation or acceptable standards for success are unique to every program. The determination of such a strategy at the initial planning phase often leads an evaluation to become a purposeful and useful program activity. A considerable amount of expertise is required to perform an adequate evaluation; yet even if outside help is sought, it should be remembered that a good evaluation is collaborative in nature, often involving an entire roster of program personnel, volunteers, and students.

National and International Associations for Voluntarism

Voluntarism, which finds expression in the volunteer and voluntary action, is an emerging field not only in the United States but in other countries as well. In 1951, an association of volunteer bureaus was formed as a constituency-based organization responding to growing needs for the exchange of information and experience to administer community-based volunteer coordination agencies in the United States and Canada. In 1966, the National Information Center on Volunteerism (NICOV) grew out of a criminal justice volunteer program in Boulder, Colorado. NICOV developed a resource collection of over 8,000 documents, including over 200 research and evaluative studies. Its major objective has been to provide technical services to the leadership of volunteer programs in all human services areas. In 1970, the National Center for Voluntary Action (NCVA) was organized to stimulate new responses to America's most pressing needs through the greater recognition, utilization, and coordination of volunteers. NCVA and some 300 Voluntary Action Centers (VAC) have served organizations that rely on volunteers to carry out their programs. In 1980, NCVA merged with NICOV to form a new organization, VOLUNTEER: The National Center for Citizen Involvement. The new organization hopes to expand on the combined strengths of the two former organizations and facilitate citizen participation of all kinds, including community development. New publications will emerge from the organization, and the enduring ones, such as the quarterly publication *Voluntary Action Leadership,* will continue.

In 1973, the Association of Voluntary Action Scholars (AVAS) was organized at Boston University and, in 1977, relocated to Boulder. This organization, which draws its membership from twenty academic fields, disciplines, and professions, has as its goal the bringing together of researchers interested in voluntarism and practitioners. AVAS publishes the quarterly journal *Voluntary Action Research,* and copublishes *Volunteer Administration* with AAVS. It also publishes a *Bibliography and Abstracts File.* Another national organization, the Association for Administration of Volunteer Services (AAVS), focuses on the generic nature of the field and the common interests shared by volunteers, regardless of the setting. This organization grants certification (called CAVS, or Certified Administrator of Volunteer Service) to administrators of volunteers.

In 1975, the above organizations appeared among seventeen major national organizations which organized the Alliance for Volunteerism. This organization, developed with funding from the Lilly Foundation, sought to encourage cooperation and unified action through communication across groups. The alliance has led to the relocation of AVAS, AAVS, and a satellite office of AVB, all of which share office space with VOLUNTEER. Conferences among AVAS, AAVS, and AVB are cosponsored, and cooperative linkages are being developed within publications, e.g., *Volunteer Administration.*

A number of universities have begun to address the need for professionally trained persons to manage volunteers. Two which have full degree programs are Antioch University (Baltimore) and Lindenwood Colleges (Washington, St. Louis, and Santa Monica). Others have developed courses in voluntarism.

The movement to stimulate interest in voluntarism, supply assistance to administrators of volunteers, and provide a research base for voluntarism can be seen elsewhere as well. In England, the Volunteer Centre was opened in 1973 in response to the Aves report. The centre has three areas of activity: collecting and disseminating information on voluntary and community involvement; advising on the training of volunteers and of the people who work with them; and discussing with statutory and voluntary authorities possibilities for extending voluntary participation. The centre has published two extensive directories, *Research into Community In-*

volvement, which cover research carried out by universities, voluntary organizations, statutory bodies, and community health councils. A British association, patterned after AVAS, has been initiated by Dr. David Zelden at the Open University in London. One of its major initiatives is international voluntarism, and it has held special sessions for European and Third World members.

Sample Job Descriptions

Midcoast humanities center job description

JOB:	Volunteer proposal writer
JOB SUMMARY:	The Midcoast Humanities Center was inaugurated 2 years ago to provide cultural opportunities to the Greater Midcoast area (200 square miles). Through the book sharing club, the film review club, and the summer theater, the center has attracted more than 200 participants. There are five full-time staff and over 50 volunteers. It is hoped that services will be expanded. However, funding is currently limited to one source, which is expected to terminate its contribution next fall. A proposal writer is expected to seek new sources of funding and apply for grant awards. He or she should be prepared to produce a proposal on a monthly basis.
SPECIFIC DUTIES:	Specific duties include understanding funding guidelines, comprehending the goals of the center, assisting in the continued development of its philosophy, identifying needs, identifying sources of funding, writing narratives, preparing a budget, and meeting funding source guidelines.
QUALIFICATIONS:	Qualifications include experience with the humanities, writing ability, and a desire to help the center expand its activities.
WORKING CONDITIONS:	The person selected will be offered the use of a desk and office equipment and will share the services of a full-time secretary. Hours are flexible. Admission to all center events and discounts on books, paintings, and sculpture are available. Meetings with board monthly.
CONTACT:	Mrs. Harold Steinbrenner at 372-9781.

Volunteer tutors needed (Bayview Educational Enrichment Program)

JOB:	Volunteer reading tutor
JOB SUMMARY:	Thirty volunteers are being sought to tutor illiterate adults. The Bayview Educational Enrichment Program (BEEP) has been in existence for 12 years, and is funded by the State Office of Education and by foundation grants. Sixty teachers are employed on a part-time basis. BEEP enrolls approximately 1000 adults per year in a variety of academic and leisure courses. Volunteers will work with one student each for an hour a week for a period of one year.
SPECIFIC DUTIES:	Responsibilities include diagnosing, placing, instructing and evaluating the student. Volunteers will select materials, methods, and techniques for instructional purposes and will file periodic reports. A 30-hour training session is made available to the volunteers.
QUALIFICATIONS:	Qualifications include willingness to learn and success on a qualifying exam. Experience in educational settings is desirable.
WORKING CONDITIONS:	Volunteers may utilize the child care facilities and cafeteria on Wednesday nights and are invited to the annual volunteer banquet. Numerous skill training opportunities are available.
CONTACT:	Mr. Joseph Jacobs Volunteer Coordinator BEEP 1200 Ridgeland Road Phone: 429–7300

Techniques

By "techniques" we mean those learning activities an instructor selects as being best suited to the needs of the learners, the objectives that have been set, and the availability of those activities. A technique, or a combination of techniques, is often employed in conjunction with devices (books, films, tapes, and so on), which will be discussed in Appendix D. The techniques discussed below[1] include lecture, panel, group discussion, buzz group, role play, process demonstration, field trip, and case study. For the sake of clarity, each technique is broken down into its structure, purpose, advantages, limitations, instructor's role, and learner's role. It is recognized that the instructor and learner may discover other advantages, limitations, and descriptions of their roles.

I Lecture
   A Structure
     A formal oral presentation in which a one-way communication pattern dominates.

[1]John A. Niemi, *The Trainer's Manual*, Girl Guides of Canada, Toronto, 1971 (revised).

B   Purpose
The primary purpose of the lecture is to impart information. The instructor may introduce a new subject or relate new material to content which has been taught before. The instructor may also give directions for a learning task to be developed by another technique.

C   Advantages
1   An appropriate technique when the particular information is not available by other means.
2   Valuable for presenting material which must be organized in a certain manner for a special group.

D   Limitations
1   Learner has no opportunity to participate.
2   Not an appropriate technique if the objective of the learning session involves the *application* of skills or information.
3   Usually complex or technical material can be handled with only limited success.

E   Instructor's role: Preparing the lecture
1   Determine its purpose.
2   Select relevant information.
3   Identify the major areas to emphasize and arrange them in logical order.
4   Support arguments with statistics and illustrations of various kinds.
5   Select audio and/or visual aids to illustrate material.
6   Decide on any reading for learners to do before the lecture. Give them the actual material to be read, a list of references, or both.
7   Preferably, use short sentences and simple language.
8   Summarize the main points.
9   Give illustrations that enable learners to relate material to their experiences.
10   Suggest other sources of information (for example, books and films) for further study of the topic.

F   Instructor's role: Giving the lecture
1   Try to engage the attention of the class at the start through an interest-catching opening, e.g., a humorous story of a personal experience related to the topic.
2   By your tone and manner, create an atmosphere in which your audience will become receptive to your ideas.
3   Avoid reading the entire presentation. You should know your subject well enough to use your notes only as a guide and a source of direct quotations.
4   Speak clearly, enunciating carefully.
5   Adjust your rate of speaking to your material and your audience, giving them time to assimilate the ideas. Generally speaking, simple, nontechnical material can be presented

more quickly than material of a complex technical nature. Also, if your audience has prior knowledge of your topic, you can usually proceed at a faster pace.

    6 Avoid mannerisms (shuffling your feet, making faces) which might distract the attention of your audience.

    7 Put into operation steps 8–10 under "Preparing the Lecture."

    8 Encourage learners to ask questions.

  G Learner's role

    1 Prepare by doing the assigned reading and thinking carefully about the topic.

    2 Listen attentively to ideas presented.

    3 Avoid behavior that distracts instructor and other learners.

    4 Take notes on major ideas, suggested further reading, and so on.

    5 Consider how the information might be used.

    6 Ask questions about unclear points.

    7 Integrate new information into one's own experience,

II Panel

  A Structure

An informal presentation in which a number of experts discuss an assigned topic which is coordinated by a moderator.

  B Purpose

Like a lecture, the panel is primarily designed to present specific knowledge. However, this knowledge is a composite of information possessed by experts or by persons whose experience qualifies them to speak with authority.

  C Advantages

    1 A variety of views held by qualified people can be communicated in an informal manner to learners, who will thereby enjoy a new learning experience.

    2 Frequently, panel members stimulate each other and learners to produce new ideas or to grasp new relationships among ideas.

  D Limitations

    1 A systematic presentation of information is rarely possible through this informal, conversational approach. However, the situation can be helped considerably if the moderator sums up the contributions of members and prods panel members and learners to raise questions.

    2 Ill-informed or irresponsible panel members can drastically curtail learning, as can an ineffective moderator.

  E Moderator's role: Preparing the panel

    1 Select four to six qualified persons and give each one an assignment.

      2 Meet with panel members to brief them, explore possible questions on which members might base their remarks, and set time limits.

      3 Tactfully suggest that members undertake research on the topic to prepare themselves for the panel.

      4 Decide on any reading for learners to do. Give them the actual material to be read, a list of references, or both.

F Moderator's role: Conducting the panel

      1 Briefly outline the topic to be discussed.

      2 Introduce panel members to learners in a manner designed to establish a relaxed, informal climate.

      3 Guide discussion by asking questions, prodding others to raise questions, and making comments, thus securing participation of members.

      4 Maintain a neutral position, but clarify issues or keep discussion on the track, as needed.

      5 Summarize both during discussion and at the end.

G Expert's (panel member's) role: Preparing for panel

      1 Carefully read and think about topic.

      2 Consult with other panel members beforehand to avoid misunderstandings or duplication of information.

      3 Plan to restrict one's remarks in order to keep within the time limit assigned to each panel member.

H Participating in panel

      1 Present ideas in an informal, relaxed manner.

      2 When making contribution or reacting to questions, keep responses short and to the point.

      3 Avoid monopolizing discussion.

      4 Entertain opposing views without showing hostility.

      5 Assist moderator to make a summary.

I Learner's role

      1 Prepare oneself by doing any assigned reading and thinking carefully about topic.

      2 Give close attention to ideas presented by speakers.

      3 Take notes on major ideas.

      4 Ask questions on unclear or incomplete points.

      5 Determine how information might be used.

      6 Integrate new information into one's own experience.

III Group discussion

  A Structure

    The group discussion technique requires the instructor to guide a group of learners to engage in purposeful dialogue on a mutually selected topic.

  B Purpose

    In general, to provide learners with an opportunity to learn from each other by discovering topics of mutual interest, by sharing information and opinions, and by identifying and exploring problems and possible solutions.

C   Advantages
1   Group discussion encourages active participation by learners in the teaching-learning process.
2   The experience of presenting ideas to a group and getting the benefits of its response helps learners to clarify and expand those ideas.
3   From the reaction of the group to their ideas, learners will gain insight into their own behavior, especially where there is a climate of mutual acceptance.
4   By developing their ability to work in a group, learners will acquire self-confidence in that role.

D   Limitations
1   Technique should not be universally applied, because not all topics lend themselves to group discussion.
2   Technique is practical only for small groups, i.e., not more than twenty persons.
3   Technique requires all learners to have a specific level of knowledge in order to contribute meaningfully to discussion.
4   Rambling, unproductive discussion, or discussion dominated by a few members, may result when learners are unaware of their responsibilities or unwilling to fulfill them.

E   Instructors role: Preparing for discussion
1   Guide group to select topic for discussion, with regard to relevance, appropriateness, and so on.
2   Decide on any reading for learners to do before the group discussion. Give them the actual material to be read, a list of references, or both.
3   Compose beforehand questions that will stimulate discussion sessions and make learners aware of them. (May link questions to specific pages or chapters in reading material.)
4   Explain to learners their individual responsibilities in group discussion, e.g., willingness to listen to others and respect for their opinions.

F   Instructor's role: Handling the discussion
1   Present topic to be discussed, using visual aids where appropriate.
2   Solicit group reaction to a tentative outline for them to follow.
3   Encourage *all* learners to participate, discourage domination by one or more individuals, and solicit responses from timid persons or those holding minority opinions.
4   Guide group to stick with topic unless there is a clear reason or desire to deviate from it.

5 Observe verbal and nonverbal signs (e.g., facial expressions) as evidence that learners are confused or in disagreement.

6 Clarify any confusion or disagreement as it arises and then make sure that discussion resumes.

7 Avoid making speeches or taking sides on an issue.

8 Take notes, or have recorder take notes, to use when presenting summaries during discussion and at the end.

G Learner's role

1 Assist instructor to select topic.

2 Help determine goals and procedures for discussion.

3 Prepare for discussion by doing any assigned reading and by thinking carefully about the topic.

4 Take responsibility for making discussion meaningful by contributing relevant ideas and experiences.

5 Seek clarification of unclear points.

6 Recognize rights of other members by listening carefully to them, respecting their views, and so on.

7 Assist in summarizing important items discussed and judging how they could be related to the course.

IV Buzz group

A Structure

A technique which enables full participation by having the instructor divide learners into small groups consisting of three to six members. Generally, 6 to 10 minutes are allotted for discussion.

B Purpose

The smaller, more intimate buzz group allows learners to hold brief, informal discussions of assigned topics or to concentrate, as a group, on a specific problem. It is important that members have a certain background of information; otherwise, they will find themselves sharing ignorance or misconceptions.

C Advantages

1 It is possible for a large audience to gain, in a short time, a variety of opinions on a topic by seeking suggestions from the smaller buzz groups.

2 A large number of questions and recommendations can be formulated by buzz groups in a short time.

3 Some learners, especially shy ones, find it easier to participate in a small group of three to six members than in a large group.

4 The structure of the buzz group makes it possible for the instructor to observe individual learners closely and to gain information about their needs and interests. Such information will assist the instructor in preparing future presentations with learners.

D Limitations
  1 The time limit imposed by the buzz group makes it impossible for new material to be presented or for complex issues to be discussed.
  2 The technique cannot be used in a room with fixed chairs.
  3 The time limit may curtail discussion at an important stage, leaving members of the buzz group frustrated.
E Instructor's role
  1 Explain to a large group of learners the purpose of the buzz group.
  2 Divide learners into buzz groups of three to six members.
  3 Encourage members to become acquainted with each other.
  4 Suggest that each buzz group arrange, formally or informally, for a recorder (scribe) to write and, later, to report its findings to the entire group.
  5 With learners, select one or two tasks and set a time limit of 6–10 minutes.
  6 Visit each buzz group in case learners need assistance.
  7 Give buzz groups a 2-minute warning before reassembling as a large group.
  8 Request each recorder to report significant contributions of his or her buzz group, avoiding duplication of points made by previous recorders.
  9 Allow other members to make additional comments or a minority report.
  10 Discuss with learners significant ideas emerging from the discussion and summarize them on a chalkboard or transparency.
  11 Suggest further study or action based on discussion.
F Learner's role
  1 Assist instructor to select topic.
  2 Become acquainted with other members of buzz group.
  3 Select recorder.
  4 Define or restate topic, when necessary, so that all members understand their tasks.
  5 Contribute ideas on topic and suggest how to solve problems.
  6 Listen carefully to others and respect their views.
  7 Judge value of information exchanged and propose ways to employ it.
V Role play
  A Structure
  A presentation in which the emphasis is on the specific roles assigned by the instructor and spontaneously portrayed by the actors (learners). They do not play "themselves," but assume

the roles of other individuals, e.g., those caught up in a con-
flicting situation.

B   Purpose
Role play helps the actors and others understand the behavior
of individuals when confronted by a certain problem, especially when the actors first assume the role of one protagonist
and then switch to the opposing role. Role play is not entertain-
ment but a means to facilitate learning.

C   Advantages
1   Role play provides the learner with an actual problem situation to act out, analyze, and discuss.
2   Role play gives both instructor and learners a broader understanding of human behavior within the context of a specific problem. As they perceive how others think and feel,
they may improve their own ability to work with people.
The actors, in particular, may gain a better understanding of
themselves.

D   Limitations
1   Role play cannot be used for complex objectives.
2   Owing to the highly emotional nature of role play, *the instructor must be well-qualified to conduct it.* For example,
the instructor may have to deal with disturbing effects upon
the actors or upon the learners in the audience.
3   The actors may lose sight of the problem as they become
increasingly involved with their roles.

E   Instructor's role
1   Explain the nature of role play as a technique.
2   Assign specific roles to volunteer actors (learners) and give
them directions.
3   Give actors time, outside of the room, to adopt the mood for
their roles.
4   Explain problem situation to rest of learners (audience) and
suggest points to watch for.
5   Signal actors to begin.
6   Curtail action after the desired aspects of the situation have
been portrayed.
7   Lead group in analyzing reasons for behaviors portrayed by
actors and possible solutions to problems.
8   Examine with the group attitudes that were not expressed.

F   Learner's role (actor)
1   Volunteer for a specific role.
2   Study carefully the role to be played.
3   Decide how to interpret the role (i.e., actions, mannerisms,
and so on) in light of the purposes of role play.
4   Play the role.
5   Participate in group discussion of role play.

     6 Share with other learners the feelings he or she had in the particular role.

  G Learner's role (audience)

     1 With instructor, choose a problem situation and decide roles to be portrayed.

     2 Observe carefully the interaction among actors in role play.

     3 Share reactions with others.

     4 Determine how to use the insights gained from the role play.

VI Demonstration

  A Structure

  A technique used by instructor to demonstrate an activity or a skill, step by step. The demonstration and verbal explanation are followed by the learners' practicing the activity or skill, e.g., a game, cooking, typing.

  B Purpose

  Demonstration permits the learner to gain a new activity or skill.

  C Advantages

     1 By showing clearly how an activity or a skill should be conducted, the demonstration may arouse the learner's interest.

     2 The learner will develop confidence by performing the activity or skill.

     3 The learner will receive immediate feedback from the instructor.

     4 The learner has an opportunity for continued practice of the activity or the skill under the instructor's direction.

  D Limitations

     1 Demonstration is suitable for only certain kinds of learning, i.e., an activity or a skill.

     2 Equipment required for the demonstration may be difficult to find and may require improvisation.

     3 Size of the group must be restricted to give all learners an opportunity for observation and practice.

  E Instructor's role: Preparing the demonstration

     1 Select the activity or the skill to be demonstrated.

     2 Decide on any reading for learners to do before the demonstration. Give them the actual material to be read, a list of references, or both.

     3 Divide the demonstration into a logical step-by-step operation.

     4 Estimate the amount of time required to demonstrate the activity or skill, so that the learner can assimilate each step.

     5 Estimate the amount of time required for the learner to practice the activity or skill.

     6 Arrange for the necessary equipment and materials.

F Instructor's role: Presenting the demonstration
    1 Mention briefly the particular activity or skill to be demonstrated.
    2 Explain each step while performing it, allowing time for questions and necessary repeat demonstrations.
    3 Suggest when and where the particular activity or skill could be used.
    4 Summarize the process demonstration.
    5 Provide each learner with sufficient time to practice each step.
    6 Observe learner's performance and correct any errors.

G Learner's role
    1 Prepare oneself by doing the assigned reading.
    2 Carefully observe process demonstration by learner.
    3 Practice steps involved in performing the activity or skill.
    4 Request instructor's assistance in steps which learner finds difficult.
    5 Determine how the activity or skill can be used in own experience.

VII Field trip

A Structure

An educational tour in which a group visits a place to observe an activity firsthand. Usually, a field trip is preceded by a preparatory meeting (e.g., lecture or group discussion), followed by a meeting designed to analyze the experience. The informal nature of the field trip gives it a flexible structure, because groups are dispersed throughout the place visited.

B Purpose

The field trip provides information to learners through a wide *variety* of experiences, such as education and visits to a learning exchange or learning center.

C Advantages
    1 The informal nature of the field trip makes it possible for learners to become better acquainted with each other.
    2 This opportunity to observe and react with a group in a supervised situation may train them to observe more closely and more accurately in the future.

D Limitation
    1 Feasibility of field trip, i.e., whether it serves a useful purpose in view of the time involved, costs, and problems of communication and administration.

E Instructor's role: Before the field trip
    1 Select with learners place to be visited as a learning experience.
    2 Make preliminary arrangements with personnel at place to be visited and arrange, where necessary, transportation, food, accommodation, and tickets of admission.

      3   Give learners data on place to be visited.

      4   Decide on any reading for learners to do before the field trip. Give them the actual material to be read, a list of references, or both.

      5   Suggest that learners make notes of their observations. (May give out a list of questions to guide learners.)

  F   Instructor's role: Field trip

      1   Meet learners at designated place and introduce them to guide and other persons. In general, look out for the welfare and comfort of group.

  G   Instructor's role: After the field trip

      1   Encourage learners to evaluate their experiences, especially to examine critically their impressions or assumptions.

      2   Summarize experiences reported by individual learners.

      3   Question group on how material might be used.

      4   Based on this experience, solicit ideas for future field trips.

  H   Guide's role: Field trip

      1   Acquaint oneself with background and interests of learners and work closely with them and the instructor.

      2   Explain points of interest or activities in terms which group can grasp, and answer questions.

  I   Learner's role

      1   Prepare oneself by doing any assigned reading and by thinking carefully about the topic.

      2   Make careful observations and notes during the trip.

      3   Seek clarification, where necessary, from guide.

      4   Analyze and interpret knowledge acquired from field trip.

      5   Integrate new information into one's own experience.

      6   Suggest future field trips, including but not limited to the followup to this trip.

VIII Case study

  A   Structure

     A technique whereby the instructor organizes a class as individuals or small groups to study a real-life situation.

  B   Purpose

     By analyzing data pertaining to a "real" situation or problem and by suggesting solutions, learners find ways to deal with other similar problems.

  C   Advantages

      1   The case study technique enables the learner to tackle a "real" situation instead of a hypothetical one.

      2   The learner develops analytical skills involved in problem solving; i.e., he or she learns to see different interpretations of a problem and different alternatives for its solution.

D Limitations
  1 Material for the case study must consist of factual information (geographical, psychological, sociological, and so on) that is accurately and fully presented.
  2 It may be difficult to find material appropriate to the situation.
E Instructor's role
  1 Carefully select detailed case study and present it to group.
  2 Assist learner to analyze data and suggest solutions to problems.
  3 Summarize learner's findings and suggest a course of action for making use of information.
F Learner's role
  1 Analyze case study material, paying close attention to elements of problems, e.g., personal conflicts.
  2 Suggest possible solutions to problems.
  3 Study other solutions offered by fellow learners.
  4 Determine how information might be used in one's own experience.

Devices

Devices include books and other printed materials, records, tapes, chalk-boards, films, filmstrips, and slides. A device, or a combination of devices, is frequently used by the instructor in conjunction with a particular technique, making it possible for material to be presented to learners through more than one sense, i.e., through sight, sound, and touch. In addition, devices provide both instructor and learners with a wide range of knowledge and experience, and can be employed in both individual and group learning. The section "Hints for Choosing and Using Devices" is followed by a section that lists the advantages and limitations of each device. It is recognized that instructor and learner alike may add to these lists as they gain experience in using devices.[1]

HINTS FOR CHOOSING AND USING DEVICES

1 There must be a *purpose* for using a device. It should illustrate or reinforce knowledge or skills being taught; e.g., a film might illustrate

[1]John A. Niemi, *The Trainer's Manual*, Girl Guides of Canada, Toronto, 1971 (revised).

cardiac massage, or a record might demonstrate how a heart should sound. Always, a device should be thought of as an integral part of a total learning experience, not as something apart from it or a gimmick. And a device should be evaluated in terms of how well it fulfills its purpose.

2   Before using a device, the instructor should inform the learners of his or her purpose. The instructor should also draw their attention to significant points presented or emphasized by means of the device; e.g., in a film on basketball, ask learners to observe the kinds of problems that can arise when an offensive team achieves a mismatch because of the difference in the height of players.

3   Such instruction provides a basis for a followup discussion after the film. The instructor will likely find that a better discussion ensues when learners have prepared themselves to deal with specific points.

4   Generally, the content of a device should be relevant to the mature learners; e.g., a book or a game designed for children should not be used with adults unless there is good reason for doing so.

5   Instructors will no doubt realize that books, pamphlets, films, tapes, filmstrips, and slides often express biases held by the authors or producers, or may be limited to one viewpoint. The situation is most likely to occur with controversial issues like sex education. Such devices may also be inaccurate or out-of-date. Instructors can avoid some of these problems by consulting reliable sources such as professional associations, libraries, and universities.

6   When using devices like charts, chalkboards, or transparencies, the instructor should include only pertinent items, being careful not to overload learners with information. Such devices should be rather simple and eye-catching, and letters should be large enough to be read by everyone. Also, they should neither be crowded together nor placed too far apart.

7   In explaining transparencies or charts, the instructor should take care not to block the view of learners.

8   The instructor should *identify* important points, i.e., make them stand out clearly, by underlining them, drawing "boxes" around them, or presenting them in color.

9   For the use of projected materials, i.e., films, filmstrips, and slides, the instructor might find this checklist helpful:
    a   Arrange for the projector and projectionist.
    b   Preview all films, filmstrips, slides to be used.
    c   Decide how they will illuminate or supplement the content being taught.
    d   Consider how ideas appearing in the film, filmstrips, or slides are to be handled—in question-and-answer periods, group discussion, and so on.
    e   Check film, filmstrip, or slides ahead of time to be sure they are complete, in good condition, and in the right order.

f Check on the availability of extra equipment, like an extension cord of the same thickness as machine cord, a spare bulb, and so on.

g Check hall or room for blackout (should be total for colored film, filmstrip, or slides), location of light switches, and outlet for projector.

h Check hall or room for ventilation and seating arrangements.

i Appoint someone to operate light switches.

j Set up equipment well ahead of time. Check to see if the projecter gates and lens are clean. Is the projector back far enough so that images fill the screen? Mark with chalk on floor the correct locations for table and screen. Then check if the screen is visible to all and that the speaker is close to the screen and well above the floor (to prevent an echo). If film or filmstrip is used, thread it through the machine and check light, focus, and sound. If slides are used, check to see if they are in the correct order and right side up.

10 After showing films, filmstrips, or slides, the instructor should leave the equipment in place until program ends. Rewinding a film or taking down a screen distracts an audience.

11 It is often a good idea to show a film, filmstrip, or slides a second time, but there must be a *purpose*, e.g., to clear up a misunderstanding, to settle an argument, or simply to study more closely the implication of a film, filmstrip, or slides.

TYPES OF DEVICES

Printed Materials

I Books
  A Advantages
    1 Learner is exposed to the thinking of good minds.
    2 Information is presented in a systematic manner.
    3 The learner can study material at his or her own rate.
  B Limitations
    1 Information contained in books may be inappropriate for a particular course.
    2 Material may be aimed at a different audience, e.g., high school students.
    3 Material may be out of date, inaccurate, or biased.
    4 Certain books may be difficult to acquire because the edition was limited.

II Pamphlets
  A Advantages
    1 The same as those relating to books.
    2 Material relating to special areas is available in condensed form, and can be read quickly.
    3 Material is usually inexpensive to acquire.

     B Limitation
       1 Same as for books.
III Homemade materials
     A Advantages
       1 Instructor can design materials to fit the special needs of learners.
       2 Learners can help to develop material that will reinforce their learning and that might be useful in future as resource material.
     B Limitations
       1 Necessary materials and equipment may not be available.
       2 Individuals with particular knowledge or skill needed to develop materials may not be available.
       3 Developing materials is time-consuming.
       4 It may be difficult to make such materials visually attractive to learners.

Audio and/or Visual Aids

  I Records
     A Advantages
       1 Make available to learners the talents of specialists.
       2 May be stopped at any point.
       3 They are portable, and record players are usually available.
     B Limitation
       1 Contain "fixed material" that cannot be changed. However, parts of a record may be appropriate to the learner's purpose.
 II Audiotapes
     A Advantages
       1 Like records, audiotapes make available to learners the talent of specialists. Also, tapes may be stopped at any point and are portable. However, tapes are more flexible than records because instructor and learners can make their own tapes (which may include live performances, radio broadcasts, and audio portions of a TV show) and then analyze them.
     B Limitations
       1 Instructor or learner may be reluctant to "perform" for a tape.
       2 Developing tapes is time-consuming.
       3 Locating a particular part on a tape may be difficult.
III Videotapes
     A Advantages
       1 Videotapes show "real" situations that could not be presented in another way (e.g., prisoners being interviewed) give closeups that show in detail such things as a portion of a painting.

2 Live material which relates directly to problems may be acquired from TV or films.

3 The nature of this medium (its appeal to several senses) is such that learners are likely to become more involved in the problem than they would through a record or an audiotape.

4 Videotapes may be used to record a class session and later analyzed for the purpose of discovering any weakness in the session.

B Limitation

1 Technical knowledge needed to operate expensive videotape equipment may not be available.

IV Films

A Advantage

1 Like videotape, films show "real" situations that could not be presented in another way, and they "involve" learners in a problem. However, films can better show an "ideal" performance (e.g., conducting a job interview) because they are carefully planned and edited, whereas videotapes are spontaneous, recording an "instant" performance.

B Limitations

1 Special equipment and a projectionist to show films cannot always be found.

2 Sometimes only part of a film is relevant to the instructor's purpose. However, it can still be useful if the instructor draws the learners' attention to important points.

3 Because the room must be dark, learners cannot take notes unless a "daylite" screen is available.

V Filmstrips

A Advantages

1 Visual images are enlarged and can be "held" indefinitely for purposes of discussion.

2 Filmstrips are compact, easily handled, and in a proper sequence.

3 They are inexpensive and require simpler and cheaper equipment than does the film.

4 They may be accompanied by records or audiotapes, chosen by the instructor to suit his or her purposes.

B Limitations

1 Filmstrips are static, lacking the movement of films and videotapes.

2 Filmstrips are also inflexible; i.e., their fixed sequence makes it impossible for the Instructor to rearrange the material.

3 It may be difficult to make filmstrips locally.

4 Because the room must be dark, learners cannot take notes.

VI Slides
  A Advantages
    1 Visual images are enlarged and can be "held" indefinitely for purposes of discussion.
    2 Unlike filmstrips, slides can be arranged in a variety of sequences in accordance with the instructor's plan.
    3 When out of date, slides can easily be discarded and replaced by new ones.
    4 They are simple and inexpensive to prepare or they can be purchased.
    5 They can be handled and stored in a small space.
    6 They can be used with records or audiotapes.
  B Limitations
    1 Like filmstrips, slides are static.
    2 They can be damaged or incorrectly projected.
    3 Because the room must be dark, learners cannot take notes.
VII Transparencies (made by instructor)
  A Advantages
    1 By making transparencies, the instructor can present material in a systematic sequence to large or small groups.
    2 The rate of projection can be controlled by the instructor.
    3 The instructor can face the audience, maintaining eye contact with them.
    4 As the room does not have to be dark, learners can take notes.
  B Limitations
    1 Transparencies are time-consuming to make, because they have to be carefully constructed with attention to the amount of information being presented, sequence, relationships to be depicted, size and clarity of writing or printing, and eye appeal.
    2 The equipment with which to make transparencies or the special overhead projector needed to display them may not be available.
VIII Photographs and other pictures
  A Advantage
    1 Like slides, photographs and other pictures can be purchased and arranged in whatever sequence the instructor chooses, can be replaced when damaged or out of date, and can be studied indefinitely by a class. With captions, photographs and other pictures are especially suited to displays (see below), and may be accompanied by records or audiotapes.
  B Limitation
    1 Like filmstrips and slides, photographs and other pictures are static. Also, they generally cannot be used "as is" with

        large groups. They require an opaque projector, which may not be available.

IX   Displays: Exhibits, bulletin boards, and models
- **A** Advantages
  1. Like slides and photographs, displays have the advantage of flexibility; i.e., they can be organized to show such procedures as completing income tax returns.
  2. Displays enable learners to study detailed material at their own rate.
- **B** Limitation
  1. Displays are static. Unless they are especially creative, commanding attention through originality and color, displays may go unnoticed.

X   Chalkboards
- **A** Advantages
  1. The flexibility of chalkboards makes them valuable devices to use with any technique. They can even be used simultaneously with a technique. For example, the instructor might illustrate a lecture by writing the major ideas on the chalkboard as he or she presents them.
  2. Chalkboards can be made visually attractive by the arrangement of material.
- **B** Limitations
  1. Chalkboards can be used only with classes of limited size.
  2. Material written on chalkboards is not "permanent."

XI   Charts and flip charts
- **A** Advantages
  1. Charts may be used to reinforce a verbal explanation or communicate statistics. Charts are especially useful for showing relationships, e.g., the roles of various individuals within the structure of an industrial organization.
  2. By using flip charts, which consist of a series of charts fastened together, the instructor can present several topics, or several aspects of a single topic, in logical sequence.
  3. Charts and flip charts can be made visually attractive by the use of color and arrangement of material.
- **B** Limitation
  1. Charts are time-consuming to make because they have to be carefully constructed with attention to amount of information being presented, sequence, relationships to be depicted, size and clarity of writing or printing, and eye appeal.

XII   Flannel graphs
- **A** Advantages
  1. Flannel graphs can be built step by step before the eyes of the class to illustrate ideas. Flannel graphs are inexpensive to make and allow for a great deal of flexibility.

      2 They can be made visually attractive by the use of color and arrangement of material.

  B Limitation

      1 They are time-consuming to make and must be made to stick properly.

XIII Multimedia

The multimedia approach, or the simultaneous use of several media (films, slides, and audiotape), has the obvious advantage of dramatizing an issue and involving the viewer in an unique way. However, it must be kept in mind that this very bombardment of the senses may be confusing, especially if the viewer is accustomed to having material presented in a linear fashion. The multimedia approach is time-consuming because of the need for coordination among the media used, and it requires expertise and a considerable amount of equipment.

XIV Radio and TV

As indicated above, radio and TV programs can be recorded on audiotapes and videotapes. Another way in which the instructor can usefully employ radio and TV is to study the guides which give information about impending programs and then to have learners listen and observe. Subsequent discussions would focus on the content and attitudes, expressed in these programs. Finally, the instructor should not overlook the possibility of having learners produce radio and TV programs of their own.

Bibliography

Americans Volunteer, ACTION (The Agency for Volunteer Service), Washington, D.C., 1975.

Anderson, John, et al.: *Training the Volunteer Coordinator: A Course Handbook,* Vancouver Volunteer Centre, British Columbia, 1977.

A Target Population in Adult Education, National Advisory Council on Adult Education, Washington, D.C., 1974.

Aves, Geraldine: *The Volunteer Worker in the Social Services,* Sage Publications, Beverly Hills, Calif., 1969.

Carter, Barbara, and Gloria Dapper: *Organizing School Volunteer Programs,* Citation Press, New York, 1974.

Cooper, Joseph D.: *How to Get More Done in Less Time,* Doubleday, Garden City, N.Y., 1971.

Cull, John G., and Richard E. Hardy: *Volunteerism: An Emerging Profession,* Charles C Thomas, Springfield, Ill., 1974.

DeBoer, John: *Let's Plan: A Guide to the Planning Process for Voluntary Organizations,* Pilgrim Press, Philadelphia, 1970.

Dekker, Tunis: "The Conference Coordinator: Educator-Administrator," *Adult Education,* Autumn 1965, pp. 37–40.

Demott, Benjamin: "The Day the Volunteers Didn't," *Psychology Today,* March 1978, pp. 23–27, 131–132.

DeRose, A., and D. Rozan: *Blueprint: A Volunteer Program,* St. Lawrence Mental Health Center, Lansing, Mich., 1973.

Drucker, Peter F.: *Management: Tasks, Responsibilities, and Practices,* Harper and Row, New York, 1974.

————: *The Effective Executive,* Harper and Row, New York, 1967.

Escobar, Joanna Sculley, and John Dougherty: *Handbook for the ESL/ABE Administrator,* Books 1-3, Northwest Educational Cooperative, Bilingual Education Service Center, Arlington Heights, Ill., 1975.

Fales, Ann W., and Alice M. Leppert: *Guidelines for Health Care Volunteers,* Church Women United, New York, 1974.

Freund, Janet: *Co-ordinators Guide, Volunteers and Volunteer Service in Schools,* Winnetka Public Schools, Winnetka, Ill., 1966.

Gagné, Robert: *The Conditions of Learning,* rev. ed., Holt, Rinehart, and Winston, New York, 1970.

Gellerman, Saul: *Motivation and Productivity,* American Management Association, New York, 1963.

Godbey, Gordon: "The Volunteer in Adult Education," unpublished doctoral dissertation, Harvard University, Cambridge, Mass., 1958.

Granger, Charles H.: "The Hierarchy of Objectives," *Harvard Business Review,* May–June, 1964, pp. 63–74.

Griffin, Bobbie: *Training and Use of Volunteer Recruiters in Adult Basic Education Programs,* Appalachian Adult Basic Education Demonstration Center, Morehead State University, Morehead, Ky., 1971.

Grotelueschen, Arden: "Evaluation," to be published by Adult Education Association and Jossey-Bass.

———— et al.: *Evaluation in Adult Basic Education: How and Why,* Interstate Printers and Publishers, Danville, Ill., 1976.

Halpin, Andrew W., and Donald B. Croft: *Organizational Climate of Schools,* Midwest Administrative Center, University of Chicago, 1963.

Herzberg, Frederick: "One More Time: How Do You Motivate Employees?" *Harvard Business Review,* January–February, 1968.

Houle, Cyril O.: *The Design of Education,* Jossey-Bass, San Francisco, 1972.

————: "The Education of Adult Education Leaders," in Malcolm S. Knowles (ed.), *Handbook of Adult Education in the United States,* Adult Education Association, Chicago, 1960.

Ilsley, Paul J.: "Voluntarism: An Action Proposal for Adult Educators," *Lifelong Learning: The Adult Years,* September 1978, pp. 8–11, 30–31.

Janowitz, Gayle: *Helping Hands: Volunteer Work in Education,* University of Chicago Press, Chicago, 1967.

Johnstone, John W. C., and Ramon J. Rivera: *Volunteers for Learning: A Study of the Educational Pursuits of American Adults,* Aldine, Chicago, 1965.

Kaslow, Florence Whiteman, et al.: *Supervision, Consultation, and Staff Training in the Helping Professions,* Jossey-Bass, San Francisco, 1977.

Katz, Robert L.: "Skills of an Effective Administrator," *Harvard Business Review,* January–February 1955.

Kidd, J.R.: *How Adults Learn,* Association Press, New York, 1977.

Knowles, Malcolm S.: *The Adult Education Movement in the United States,* Holt, Rinehart and Winston, New York, 1962.

————: *The Adult Learner: A Neglected Species,* Gulf, Houston, 1973.

————: *The Modern Practice of Adult Education: Andragogy versus Pedagogy,* Association Press, New York, 1973.

Knox, Alan B., et al.: *An Evaluation Guide for Adult Basic Education Programs,* U.S. Government Printing Office, Washington, D.C., 1972.

Leat, Diana: *Research into Community Involvement, 1974–77,* Volunteer Centre, Berkhamsted, Great Britain, 1977.

Levin, Stanley, et al.: *Handbook on Volunteers in Army Community Service.* Human Services Research Organization, Alexandria, Va., 1969.

Litwin, George H., and Robert A. Stringer, Jr.: *Motivation and Organizational Climate,* Harvard University Press, Cambridge, Mass., 1968.

Lobb, Charlotte: *Exploring Careers through Volunteerism,* Rosen Press, New York, 1976.

Loen, Raymond O.: *Manage More by Doing Less,* McGraw-Hill, New York, 1971.

Loeser, Herta: *Women, Work, and Volunteering,* Beacon, Boston, 1974.

Mager, Robert F., and Kenneth M. Beach, Jr.: *Developing Vocational Instruction,* Fearon, Palo Alto, Calif., 1967.

Maslow, Abraham: *Motivation and Personality,* Harper and Row, New York, 1970.

Mason, Robert C. "Managerial Role and Style," in Philip D. Langerman and Douglas Smith (eds.), *Managing Adult and Continuing Education Programs and Staff,* National Association for Public Continuing and Adult Education, Washington, D.C., 1979.

McGregor, Douglas: *The Human Side of Enterprise,* McGraw-Hill, New York, 1960.

Naylor, Harriet H.: *Volunteers Today: Finding, Training, and Working with Them,* Association Press, New York, 1967.

Netherton, Wendy: *Developing Student Volunteer Programs: A Handbook,* Volunteer Centre Winnipeg, Manitoba, 1977.

Niemi, John A. (ed.): *Mass Media and Adult Education,* Educational Technology Publications, Englewood Cliffs, N.J., 1971.

————: *The Trainer's Manual,* Girl Guides of Canada, Toronto, 1971.

————, and Catherine Davison: "The Adult Basic Education Teacher: A Model for the Analysis of Training," Adult Leadership, February 1971, pp. 246–248, 276.

————, and John M. Nagle, "Learners, Agencies, and Program Development in Adult and Continuing Education," in Philip D. Langerman and Douglas H. Smith (eds.), *Managing Adult and Continuing Education Programs and Staff,* National Association for Public Continuing and Adult Education, Washington, D.C., 1979.

————, and Eve M. Stone: *Voluntarism at the Crossroads: A Challenge for Adult Educators,* Conference Proceedings, Northern Illinois University, DeKalb, Ill., 1978.

O'Connell, Brian: *Effective Leadership in Voluntary Organizations,* Association Press, New York, 1976.

Odiorne, George S.: *Management by Objectives,* Pitman, Belmont, Calif., 1965.

Owens, Robert G., and Carl R. Steinhoff: *Administering Change in Schools,* Prentice Hall, Englewood Cliffs, N.J., 1976.

Patterson, Virginia C., "Characteristics and Motivational Factors of Volunteer Club Leaders in Evangelical Churches: An Analysis of Pioneer Girls' Club Leaders," unpublished doctoral dissertation, Northern Illinois University, DeKalb, Ill., 1978.

Paulson, C. F.: *A Strategy for Evaluative Design,* Teaching Research, Oregon State System of Higher Education, Monmouth, Oreg., 1970.

Pearl, Arthur, and Frank Riessman: *New Careers for the Poor,* Free Press, New York, 1965.

Pell, Arthur: *Recruiting, Training and Motivating Volunteer Workers,* Pilot, New York, 1972.

Russell, Aritha, and Jeanne DeLucio: *Volunteer Handbook: Volunteerism for the Adult Learner,* Joliet Junior College, Joliet, Ill., 1979.

Scheirer, Ivan: *People Approach,* National Information Center on Volunteerism, Boulder, Colo., 1977.

————: *Orienting Staff to Volunteers,* National Information Center on Volunteerism, Boulder, Colo., 1972.

Schien, Edgar: *Organizational Psychology,* Prentice-Hall, Englewood Cliffs, N.J., 1965.

Schindler-Rainman, Eva, and Ronald Lippitt: *The Volunteer Community: Creative Use of Human Resources,* NTL Learning Resources Corporation, Fairfax, Va., 1975.

Schmais, Aaron: *Implementing Nonprofessional Programs in Human Services,* Center for the Study of Unemployed Youth, New York University, 1967.

Schroeder, Wayne L.: "Adult Education Defined and Described," in Robert M. Smith et al. (eds.), *Handbook of Adult Education,* Macmillan, and Adult Education Association of the U.S.A., New York, 1970, pp. 25–43.

Scriven, Jolene, "How to Manage Time Better," unpublished paper presented at Northern Illinois University, DeKalb, Ill., 1977.

Smith, David Horton: *Policy Research Needs: Report of a Participative Inquiry,* Center for a Voluntary Society, Washington, D.C., 1974.

Steele, Sara: "Program Evaluation as an Administrative Concept," paper presented at AERA Annual meeting, New Orleans, Feb. 28, 1973.

Stenzel, Anne K., and Helen M. Feeney: *Volunteer Training and Development: A Manual,* Seaburg Press, New York, 1976.

Stevenson, T. H.: *Building Better Volunteer Programs,* Foundations for Voluntary Welfare, Princeton, N.J., 1971.

Suchman, Edward A.: *Evaluative Research,* Russell Sage Foundation, New York, 1977.

Tannenbaum, Robert, and Warren H. Schmidt: "How to Choose a Leadership Pattern," *Harvard Business Review,* March–April 1965, pp. 95–101.

Training Volunteer Leaders, National Council of Young Men's Christian Association, New York, 1974.

Ungerson, Bernard (ed.), *Recruitment Handbook*, Glower Press. Epping. Great Britain. 1975.

Volunteers in Education, Recruitment Leadership and Training Institute, Philadelphia, 1975.

Volunteer Leadership Development: Chapter Executive's Guide, American National Red Cross, Washington, D.C., 1972.

Williams, Roger K.: *How to Evaluate, Select, and Work with Executive Recruiters,* Cahners, Boston, 1974.

Wilson, Marlene: *The Effective Management of Volunteer Programs,* Volunteer Management Associates, Boulder, Colo., 1976.

Wolozin, Harold: *The Value of Volunteer Services in the United States,* ACTION, Department of Labor, Washington, D.C., 1975.

Working With Volunteers, Adult Education Association, Chicago, 1956.

Index